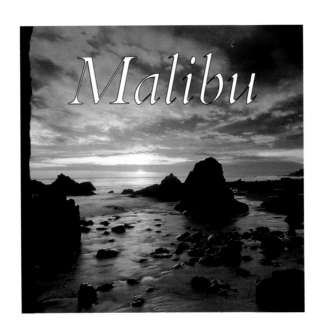

Rancho Malibu • ITS SIGNIFICANCE

In this book will be found a description of the historic Rancho Malibu, a seaside property containing over 17,000 acres of land extending along twenty-two miles of beach, within thirty minutes of Hollywood and Los Angeles.

For the first time since the days of the Spanish dons, this Rancho, an empire in itself, is being broken up and offered for sale. It is the last, and most desirable residential seashore development, in Southern California.

There is presented herein an opportunity for the discriminating buyer to secure anything from a single beach lot to a 640-acre Rancho.

Homesites, estates, beach-front property and ranchitos, the ownership of which has been sought after for years, are now for the first time available for purchase.

Every piece of property will be thoroughly protected as to surrounding land usage by intelligently drawn restrictions.

The significance in the offering of this vast property should be given thoughtful consideration by the prospective purchaser . . . that the sale, in varied units, of the Rancho Malibu, is a *liquidation*, presenting the opportunity of buying land of unduplicated appeal at sub-market prices.

Rancho Malibu is the home of the world famous Motion Picture Colony.

Marblehead Land Company

Rancho Malibu ● PERTINENT FACTORS

Enhancement of Values Inevitable

1. AREA—Approximately 17,000 acres.

2. OCEAN FRONTAGE—Approximately 22 miles.

3. EXPOSURE—The coast line of the Malibu runs in a general east and west direction, giving a southern exposure to the property.

4. SCOPE—Depth of the ranch from the beach averages one to two miles.

5. LOCATION—The Malibu fronts on Santa Monica Bay, in Los Angeles County.

6. DISTANCES—

To Los Angeles	22 miles
To Hollywood	16 miles
To Beverly Hills	12 miles
To Santa Barbara	50 miles
To Santa Monica	8 miles

7. CLIMATE—Typical Southern Californian.

8. TEMPERATURE—Ranging ten degrees warmer than Los Angeles in the winter time, due to the southern exposure, proximity to the ocean and the protection afforded by the hills to the north.

9. INVESTMENT OPPORTUNITY—The total ocean frontage available in Los Angeles County is limited to seventy-one miles. Except for the beach frontage available on the Rancho Malibu, most of the county's ocean frontage already has been disposed of and is now in use for public beaches, harbors, amusement piers, clubs, commercial uses, etc., so that the Rancho Malibu presents the last opportunity to buy close-in and desirable private beach frontage. Ocean frontage sites in other cities along Santa Monica Bay have shown a tremendous enhancement during the last eighteen years. It is proper that emphasis should be placed on the law of supply and demand as applicable to ocean frontage in Los Angeles County. The supply of beaches can never be increased in the future and the demand will necessarily continue to increase with the population. *Therefore the growing scarcity of beach property, combined with the creation of the most desirable environment to be found on the Malibu will cause a great enhancement of values.*

*Nice and
Monte Carlo,
France*

Sorrento, Italy

*Sorrento,
Italy*

With its twenty-two miles of ocean
frontage and magnificent building
sites, the Rancho Malibu is
immediately classified with the
grandeur of famous European
watering places.

*Amalfi,
Italy*

THE WORLD FAMOUS

Rancho Malibu

17000 acres...22 miles ocean frontage

MARBLEHEAD LAND COMPANY

Malibu

California's Most Famous Seaside Community

Marian Hall

Photographs by Nick Rodionoff, *et al.*

Malibu: California's Most Famous Seaside Community
Copyright © 2005 by Marian Hall

Designed by Amy Inouye, www.futurestudio.com

First edition
10 9 8 7 6 5 4 3 2 1

ISBN 1-883318-56-4 (hardcover edition)
ISBN 1-883318-59-9 (paperbound edition)

Library of Congress Cataloging-in-Publication Data

Hall, Marian.
  Malibu : California's most famous seaside community / by Marian Hall ; photographs by Nick Rodionoff, et al.-- 1st ed.
      p. cm.
  Summary: "Longtime Malibu resident Marian Hall relates the legend, lore and history of one of America's most beautiful coastal enclaves—from the earliest explorers who communed with the Chumash Indians, to today, showing and telling why it has become among the most-expensive beach and mountain property in the world, home to the rich, the famous, the party-folk and the quiet types, up-and-comers and old-timers"—Provided by publisher.
  Includes bibliographical references.
  ISBN 1-883318-56-4 (hardcover : alk. paper) -- ISBN 1-883318-59-9 (paperbound : alk. paper)
  1. Malibu (Calif.)--History. 2. Malibu (Calif.)--Social life and customs. 3. Folklore--California--Malibu. 4. Malibu (Calif.)--Biography. I. Rodionoff, Nick. II. Title.

  F869.M27H35 2005
  979.4'93--dc22

                          2005015771

Printed in China

ANGEL CITY PRESS
2118 Wilshire Boulevard #880
Santa Monica, California 90403
310.395.9982
www.angelcitypress.com

To My Family

Lem, Jenny, Peter, Ben and Adam

and all our "Happy Days" in Malibu

"Yon boundless ocean
is the best symbol of eternity."

—FREDERICK HASTINGS RINDGE

In 1898, the last private owner of the Malibu Rancho, businessman Frederick Hastings Rindge wrote *Happy Days in Southern California,* a book that came from his heart, describing with pure joy and love the Malibu that he knew so well. He celebrated the air, the sun, the moon, the stars, the wind, the sand, the sea, the flowers, the trees, the birds, the bees, the mountains, the streams and even the happy *vaqueros*. His was unparalleled passion, the kind that comes from living and loving a place, the kind that will not allow you to overlook one tiny bit of the nature around you.

> *It is delightful to live in such a place that, when the prevailing winds blow, one can send one's mind in the direction whence the wind comes, and realize that it sweeps over a pure expanse of the ocean, or over the righteous aromatic mountains; and not to be obliged to breathe the air that is blown over an iniquitous city or over some malodorous low-lands.*
> —Frederick Hastings Rindge

Today, Malibu is a state of mind but, just as importantly, it is a way of life. That way of life inspires people from all over the world to attempt to take the spirit of Malibu home with them, be it to the tiniest townships in America or the popular boulevards of international cities. Capturing the way of life and the state of mind means experiencing Malibu to the fullest. In this book we will take a spin north on Highway 1, the famed Pacific Coast Highway, locally known as "PCH," the road that spans this strip of California coast and has been an important part of its history. You'll view PCH as the locals do, thanks to photographer Nick Rodionoff and others who have cast their lenses on this twenty-seven-mile strip of paradise. You will read about the rich history and lore of Malibu—tales of the Chumash Indians, the early Spanish explorers, Spanish land grants, the early settlers and the Rindge family's fight to preserve Malibu as a private oasis. You will see how Hollywood created Malibu Colony in 1926, when stars built beach cottages on the first strip of Malibu Beach that was leased, just north of Malibu Creek. And you will visit those many beaches along the coast where surfers have ridden the waves since the 1930s and where the real Gidget shared her sand with movie-goers in the 1960s. By the time you venture north from Las Flores, La Costa and Carbon Beaches, follow the Backbone Trail through Malibu's shady canyons to the sunny highlands of dramatic Boney Ridge and visit the white sands of historic Carrillo Beach—you will be captivated by the essence of Malibu.

It is my hope that these pages will bring you the romance of the place—a romance with whatever you fancy, be it the beauty of the landscape, the country charm, the challenges of nature or simply those sparkling Malibu days and those incomparable Malibu sunsets.

—MARIAN HALL, 2005

"In this good country you need not fear
to take a deep, long breath.
Surely 'tis life to live in this wonder-land!"

—FREDERICK HASTINGS RINDGE

1

RANCHO TOPANGA MALIBU SEQUIT:
A BRIEF HISTORY

"The happiest thought of all thoughts

in connection with this beautiful land is that

only Heaven is more beautiful."

—Frederick Hastings Rindge

"*We found a memorial* of these our first predecessors—an ancient cave-dwelling,

The earliest recorded history of Malibu was penned in the journals of the Spanish explorers who visited the coast of North America. Sailing from Navidad, Mexico, in his caravel, Juan Rodriguez Cabrillo dropped anchor off the Malibu coast on October 10, 1542, and claimed the land for the king of Spain. The point of land is known today as Malibu Lagoon, where Malibu Creek meets the Pacific Ocean. The Spaniards gazed upon a vista like none they had ever seen: dramatic stretches of sand adjacent to rambling foothills with craggy mountains as a backdrop. Inhabiting the beautiful land was a spirited group of native people who had named the site of their seaside village *Humaliwo* ("where the surf sounds loudly").

The Chumash Indians
(Malibu: 5000 B.C. to 1830 A.D.)

The Chumash Indians who greeted the explorers were the earliest inhabitants of the land we know today as Malibu, a fact substantiated by Chumash petroglyphs dating from 5000 B.C. Cabrillo set sail north three days after he arrived, but not before taking careful note of the people he found there. Cabrillo's journal explains that the houses of the Chumash "are well constructed, round like an oven, spacious and fairly comfortable; light enters through a hole in the roof. Their beds are on frames and they cover themselves with skins and shawls. In the middle of the floor they make a fire for cooking seeds, fish, and other foods—for they eat everything boiled or roasted." Diaries note that Chumash men wore only a string at their waistline, but were otherwise naked, and that women were "fairly good looking."

The Chumash traveled the coast via *tomol*, a large plank canoe, which was useful for trading, and used the peaceful water of the lagoon to launch their canoes. In 1775, Father Pedro Font, who wrote the record of Captain Juan Bautista de Anza's expedition to California, described the construction of a *tomol*: "They are very carefully made of several planks, which they work with no other tools but their shells and flints. They join them at the seams by sewing them with very strong thread, which they have, and fit the joints with pitch. Some of the launches are decorated with little shells and all are painted red with hematite." The Chumash demonstrated their innovation and artistic talents by creating stone bowls, baskets so tightly woven that when covered with asphaltum from the sea, they could hold water, flints, arrowheads and spearheads, rope, knives, jewelry, fishhooks and tools. Although historians report that the Chumash inhabited Malibu until 1830, the legacy of these native people still prevails in the beautiful names of nearby canyons, beaches and mountains that can be traced to the words of the Chumash: Malibu. Topanga. Soston. Zuma.

The Tapia Family
(Malibu: 1802 to 1857)

In 1775, more than two hundred years after Cabrillo dropped anchor at Malibu, Juan Bautista de Anza was sent from Mexico by King Charles III of Spain to settle in California. He brought more than two hundred fifty men, women and children, almost seven hundred horses and

with its smoke-darkened ceiling and its heaps
of debris . . . the remains of a thousand feasts."

—FREDERICK HASTINGS RINDGE

more than three hundred head of cattle. On February 22, 1776, he established a camp at Malibu Creek. One of de Anza's men, Felipe Santiago Tapia, brought his son José Bartolomé Tapia (born in Culican, Mexico) on the expedition. The Tapia family moved on, to northern California, but in 1802, José, now an accomplished soldier and farmer, requested use of the land he had seen as a child. His wish granted by the Spanish commander in Santa Barbara, José Tapia was awarded a land-use concession so he and his family could live on the rancho and work the land. Tapia became the first person to settle and graze cattle on *Rancho Malibu Topanga Sequit,* and in 1802 was awarded one of a very few formal land grants made by the Spanish governors before the Mexican Revolution in 1821. By virtue of his use of the land, he amassed a small fortune and was soon known as Don Bartolo Tapia. He built an adobe house, a mill and corrals on the north side of Malibu Creek, an area surrounded by a vineyard and vast grazing grasslands for his horses and six hundred head of cattle.

Unfortunately, as was the practice in the days of Spanish-controlled California land, Tapia had never been given official documents. Later, between 1822 and 1846, after the Mexican-Spanish revolution, Mexican land grants confirmed many of the early Spanish concessions. But Tapia's was never confirmed, which would eventually become a serious problem for his descendants. Don Bartolo died in 1824 and willed the rancho to his wife, Doña Maria, and their son, Tiburcio.

A successful merchant importing goods to

California, in 1831 Tiburcio became *alcalde*, or mayor, of *Pueblo de la Reina de Los Angeles*, the pueblo of the Queen of the Angels, known simply as Los Angeles. After his term ended, Tiburcio was named a Superior Court judge, and was alcalde for three more terms, in 1836, 1839 and 1844. So successful was Tiburcio in his business pursuits that he was acknowledged as the richest man in Los Angeles, the most successful merchant and, indeed, the only native merchant. When the United States took over California in 1846, many contemporaries believed that Tiburcio had buried his wealth at his Malibu rancho or on his other property, *Rancho Cucamonga*.

Leon Victor Prudhomme worked as manager of Tiburcio's Malibu rancho, helping the widow Doña Maria. A Frenchman, Prudhomme had a special interest in growing grapes. He became a Mexican citizen and eventually married Tiburcio's sixteen-year-old daughter, Maria Merced Tapia, the granddaughter of Don Bartolo and Doña Maria. In 1848, a year after Tiburcio's death, his family sold the rancho to Maria and her husband for four hundred pesos: two hundred in cash and two hundred in groceries and wine. However, Prudhomme had a difficult time clearing title to *Rancho Topanga Malibu Sequit* since no documents existed to prove that the land had actually been granted to Don Bartolo. Finally, tired of all the legal battles with the United States Land Commission and disappointed that the real estate boom of Gold Rush days was over, he sold the property via a quitclaim deed to Irishman Matthew Keller in 1857.

MATTHEW KELLER, left, is shown with two prominent Los Angeles leaders and Southern California land-owners, Captain Phineas Banning (center) of San Pedro and John J. Hollister of Point Conception, near Santa Barbara. Banning was president of Pioneer Oil Company and owned a freight forwarding house which Keller used to ship his wines to his "wine house" in San Francisco. Like Keller, most men who owned other ranchos had homes in the Pueblo. Circa 1858.

The Keller Family
(Malibu: 1857 to 1892)

Matthew Keller had arrived in Los Angeles in 1850 and opened a general merchandise store on Los Angeles Street. He bought the property where Union Station now stands, determined to be one of Los Angeles's pioneer vintners. Besides building his family home, Keller planted a vineyard and orchard, and imported orange seeds from Central America. Establishing himself quickly as a respected businessman in the city, he became active on the Los Angeles Board of Supervisors, the city council, the boards of Pioneer Oil Company, the Los Angeles and San Pedro Railroad Company and various banks. The Irishman's prestige grew and he was soon known as Don Mateo. Although he owned many pieces of property in Los Angeles, his purchase of the Malibu rancho from Prudhomme was perhaps his best buy. For a quitclaim that cost fourteen hundred dollars, little more than ten cents an acre, Keller acquired 13,315 acres of the coastal, mountain and canyon land that comprised the entire rancho. The land extended twenty miles, from Las Flores Canyon almost to the Ventura County line and at its widest point spanned only two and one-half miles. The Tapia family and other settlers had lived on and farmed the land during the twenty years it took for Tiburcio to attempt to clear title, but now, to gain his own free title, Keller obtained a court order to evict all of them.

Finally after a decade of Keller's wheeling and dealing, on August 29, 1872, President Ulysses Grant granted him *Rancho Topanga Malibu Sequit* and named Keller the only official recorded owner of the Malibu property, negating any of the land's Spanish and Mexican history. His new acquisition was defined by a United States government survey to stretch from the area named *Topanga* on the southeast, along the Pacific Ocean to a point called *Mugu* on the northwest, to the range of rocks in the northeast that adjoined the ranchos of *Las Virgenes, Triunfo, Santa Ysabel* and *Conejo*. Three square leagues. The rancho was an abundant and beautiful piece of property that would one day become some of the most

LOS ANGELES VINEYARD. Matthew Keller planted a vineyard and fruit trees on his property in Los Angeles, where Union Station now stands. By 1852 he established his winery, producing claret, port, sherry, Madeira and white wines under the label of Los Angeles Vineyard and brandy under the label, Rising Sun. The products were distributed throughout California and Keller was the first vintner to sell California wines on the East Coast.

desirable land in the world.

Keller and his family built a large country house in Malibu Canyon where they lived along with the overseer of the ranch and the *vaqueros* who worked the land. The Kellers lived in the canyon until 1875 when Keller leased the rancho as grazing land to cattleman Louis Sentous and his brother. Their herd would remain on the property until a decade after Keller's death.

When Matthew Keller died in 1881, his son Henry, who had been educated in France and barely spoke English, returned to Los Angeles. He inherited the beautiful coastal property from his father. Though it was to be his when he came of age, Henry did not take possession until 1891 after a long probate. Less than a year later, he sold *Rancho Topanga Malibu Sequit,* to the final private owner of the rancho, the wealthy Frederick Hastings Rindge, for ten dollars an acre. In 1899 Henry Keller returned to Malibu and bought the property owned by Henry and Cordelia Swinney in Solstice Canyon, where he built a cabin.

May and Frederick H. Rindge
(Malibu: 1892 to 1905)

No American family is more inextricably linked to the history of Malibu than the Rindges. Frederick Hastings Rindge married Michigan schoolteacher Rhoda May Knight in 1887 and the couple immediately moved from Cambridge, Massachusetts, to Los Angeles to raise their family and build their fortune. The Harvard-educated Rindge had inherited more than two million dollars from his family estate, so he invested heavily in California where he founded Conservative Life Insurance Company (today known as Pacific Mutual), was a vice president of Union Oil Company and a director of Los Angeles Edison Electric Company (which would later become Southern California Edison). Eventually history would record that Rindge had made many wise investments both in California and Mexico, and that he also was a charitable man who had donated funds for the city hall, a school and a library in his hometown of Cambridge. Deeply religious, Rindge, who had established the first church at Harvard University, founded Santa Monica's First Methodist-Episcopal Church and another in Yreka, California, where his sister-in-law, Emily, lived.

The Rindges built two homes in Los Angeles before moving to the seaside bluffs of Santa Monica in 1891 where they constructed a large home on Ocean Avenue across from the current site of the famed Miramar Hotel. He had been searching all of his adult life for a place in the United States as beautiful as the rivieras of Italy and France, that he had seen in his travels—a place where he could settle and build a country home for his family. In 1892, Rindge's dream came true when he purchased *Rancho Topanga Malibu Sequit*. Rindge conveyed his love of Malibu and the spiritual satisfaction it provided him in his 1898 book *Happy Days in Southern California:*

FREDERICK HASTINGS RINDGE

Here in these almost hallowed hills, in this calm and sweet retreat, protected from the wearing haste of city life, an ennobling stillness makes the mind ascend to heaven.

When Rindge took possession of the rancho in 1892, most of the land was used as a cattle and grain ranch. In time, Rindge increased the ranch from 13,315 acres to more than 17,000 acres, bringing his total investment to about $300,000 (based on a 1905 appraisal).

The ranch house was built in Malibu Canyon just below where Serra Retreat is located today, and it became the weekend and vacation retreat for Frederick, May and their three children, Samuel, Frederick Jr., and Rhoda. The structure was tragically destroyed by a brush fire in 1903. Two years later, on August 29, 1905, tragedy struck the family again when Frederick Hastings Rindge died unexpectedly at age forty-eight, while visiting Yreka, a town near the northern border of California.

RANCHO MALIBU GATE was locked by the Rindge family to preserve the privacy of their land. This rare photo shows the gate as it looked in 1906. The Rindge family posted no-trespassing signs to discourage squatters and homesteaders who had been settling in the Santa Monica Mountains beginning in the 1880s. Armed guards sometimes chased off unwanted trespassers. Frederick Rindge provided a key to some of the homesteaders to the north.

MAY KNIGHT RINDGE

She was labeled
"Queen of
the Malibu"

May Knight Rindge
(Malibu: 1905 to 1941)

After her husband's death, May Knight Rindge took over the management of her Malibu Ranch. Her determination to preserve and protect the family's property became legendary. *The Los Angeles Times* nicknamed her "Queen of the Malibu." Known to pack a pistol when riding horseback around her rancho with her guards, she warded off trespassers, travelers, campers and homesteaders who were increasingly populating the mountains, poaching livestock and posing the threat of starting wildfires.

Because the Interstate Commerce Commision decreed that only one railroad could be built on any single route, as early as 1903 Frederick Rindge had planned to build a private railroad along the beach in Malibu to prevent the Southern Pacific from linking its coastal tracks from Santa Barbara to Santa Monica. True to her late husband's plan, beginning in 1906 May Rindge laid fifteen miles of standard-gauge track for her Hueneme, Malibu and Port Los Angeles Railroad, which was completed in 1908, making her the first female president of a railroad. Her train was used to transport supplies, grain, hides and other products of the ranch to the Rindge's private pier (where they then were shipped to San Pedro), but her greatest accomplishment was foiling the plans of the Southern Pacific.

Although May successfully fought the giant Southern Pacific, she was thwarted when the state and county attempted to put a road through her pristine rancho. In 1917 May closed the private road that led to the ranch, meaning the land was only accessible via the beach at low tide. Stymied homesteaders—who had become her nemesis—petitioned and the courts ordered her to reopen the road. Instead, she erected high fences around the borders with armed guards riding the border of the rancho. Her long battle to save her property began. Waging her war on land was one thing, but her battle in the courts was another—an expensive fight that took her not just to the state's highest courts, but twice to the United States Supreme Court. And she lost each step of the way. In 1925 a superior court judge ruled against May Rindge and gave the state permission to lay a highway through the center of her rancho. By 1929 automobiles were driving into her haven.

In the midst of this fight to maintain the privacy of her ranch, May Rindge had other concerns that would overwhelm most people. In need of income to pay taxes and fight legal battles, she founded the Marblehead Land Company (named after the island in Massachussetts where the family had lived and vacationed) in 1921 to own and operate the Malibu Ranch. As another source of revenue, she had founded and built the famed Malibu Potteries in 1926. The pier and the railroad right-of-way became part of the Marblehead Land Company which issued bonds in 1928 to develop Malibu. She also started construction on her fifty-room dream castle on "Laudamus Hill" in 1928, but it was never completed. The combination of a huge inheritance tax after Frederick's death, heavy land taxes throughout the years, the expensive legal battles with the county and state, and the Depression of 1929, all contributed to May's greatest defeat. By 1936 the Marblehead Land Company declared bankruptcy, and the bondholders took control. Howard Bonsall became president of the Marblehead Land Company. Realtor Louis T. Busch and Bonsall worked together to subdivide and sell Malibu land. May Rindge died in February 1941 at age seventy-six.

May's daughter, Rhoda Rindge Adamson and her husband Merritt Adamson built a beach house on land her mother had given her at Vaquero Point in 1928. It became the Adamson family's year-round residence in 1936. After her mother's death Rhoda took charge of the ranch and the Marblehead Land Company, leading it back to solvency by 1952. Upon Rhoda's death in 1961, her son, Merritt, Jr., and his sisters inherited the future of Malibu.

SPRING ROUNDUP finds May Rindge, far right, with her friend Frances Whitsett picnicking in Zuma Canyon. Also pictured are Francisco Ruiz (kneeling, with beard), landscaper Dewitt Norris (seated in vest and tie) and several *vaqueros*. Circa 1909.

"Early in the morning some fifteen men mounted and assembled at the ranch house and, starting forth, hunt the hills and valleys in a twenty-mile area for cattle, and drive them all to a certain vale, where there is a large sycamore-log corral.

Then the men ride in and cut out the cows that have calves, which are now about to be branded."

——FREDERICK H. RINDGE, 1898

AN AFTERNOON RIDE. May Rindge entertains guests at her Malibu rancho on a Sunday afternoon. From left to right: May Rindge, her son Frederick Jr.; Jessie Mathieson, a friend of Rhoda; May's daughter Rhoda, three unidentified friends and May's son Samuel. Note the formal dress of those Victorian days. Circa 1908.

ZUMA CANYON was the site of the working headquarters where the *vaqueros* of *Rancho Malibu* lived. The feed, barns, corrals, horses, wagons and all the needs of a working ranch were located there.

TRACKS ON MALIBU BEACH. Hueneme, Malibu, and Port Los Angeles Railway, a standard-gauge rail line with a small gasoline engine and a few flatcars was incorporated in 1905 by the Rindge family. Starting at the pier, the rail line was granted a two-hundred-foot-wide strip along the beaches of the entire ranch. The fifteen miles of track extended from what is now called Las Flores to just west of Encinal Canyon.

MALIBU PIER. The Rindge family built Malibu Pier in 1905 to ship and receive supplies to and from the ranch. This photo shows the unloading of tracks for the railroad. The Rindge family used the pier until 1934, when it was leased out to Al Camp and Captain Frank Wilson for sports fishing.

THE MILLION-DOLLAR RAILWAY was paid for by May Rindge. A huge investment in 1908, the price was worth it to May, who was desperate to keep the Southern Pacific off her Malibu land. The line was used to transport supplies around the ranch until 1920. The highlight of this train ride was the spectacular one-hundred-fifteen-foot trestle that spanned Paradise Cove. Note the cattle on Point Dume in the distance.

MALIBU DAM, located about two and one-half miles from the ocean in Malibu Canyon, spans one hundred forty feet across Malibu Creek and is one hundred two feet high. It was originally built in 1924 to provide the water supply for the Rindges' ranch, and would eventually provide water for Malibu Colony. This photo was taken after a storm in the late 1940s.

The dam continues to be the center of controversy. The State Department of Fish and Game and environmentalists want to remove it to protect the steelhead trout habitat, while the descendants of the Rindges and historians are fighting to save Malibu Dam as a California historical point of interest.

THE RINDGES' MALIBU CASTLE was a tile-roofed Mediterranean mansion designed by noted Los Angeles architect Stiles Clements, situated on a twenty-six-acre knoll in Malibu Canyon overlooking the creek. May Rindge started construction of this fifty-room palatial structure in 1928. Her own Malibu Potteries company provided tile for use in most of the rooms throughout the structure, which included suites for her family, a baronial hall, a tiled living room, a music room (large enough to seat the Los Angeles Philharmonic Orchestra), an oak library and a tower with 360-degree views of the countryside and coast. She had invested a half-million dollars, but construction was abandoned in 1936 when her Marblehead Land Company declared bankruptcy. She never completed the manse.

THE MALIBU POTTERIES was created by May Rindge in 1926 to help bring revenue after the drain of all the legal battles to keep Malibu private. May's Marblehead Land Company made the initial investment of $250,000. Tile was in demand for the popular Mediterranean-style homes being built in Southern California and, fortunately for May, Malibu had the perfect soil for making tile clay. The Potteries were built on the beachfront south of the pier and employed one hundred twenty-five people. The showroom and warehouse were on Larchmont Boulevard in Los Angeles. Although the Potteries facility was rebuilt after being partially burned by a fire, May Rindge was forced to close the company in 1932 due to an economy hard hit by the Depression.

Architect Stiles Clements designed the rambling Spanish Colonial Adamson House, which features tiles from the family's Malibu Potteries. The view of a sparkling blue ocean, the Mediterranean and tropical foliage with large sycamore trees and the special touch of colorful Malibu Potteries pots creates a beautiful garden.

During World War II, the United States Coast Guard patrolled Malibu's coastline constantly. The Adamson pool house served as Command Post No. 5 for the seven outlying beach patrol stations from Point Mugu to Big Rock. Hutlets were built to house the personnel who patrolled by walking the beaches every night and scanning the horizon by day. Each night strict blackout laws for both automobile and residential lights were enforced.

Adamson House is listed as No. 966 on the National Register of Historic Places, preserved for posterity by the efforts of the Malibu Historical Society, Judge John Merrick and Ronald Rindge, the great-grandson of Frederick and May. Their determination saved an intrinsic part of Malibu's past, a mansion and grounds that were once slated to be replaced by a parking lot for Surfrider Beach. In 1981 the Malibu Lagoon Museum was formed with Frederick May as president. It is managed with the help of volunteer docents, who give tours of the house. Weddings are held on weekends in the gardens, which are tended by the California Department of Parks and Recreation.

THE ADAMSON HOUSE is situated on thirteen acres at Vaquero Point. Built by the Rindge's only daughter, Rhoda Agatha Rindge Adamson and her husband Merritt Huntley Adamson, the house sits on land her mother had given them as an engagement present in 1928. The couple used this property as a beach house until 1936 when they moved from Hancock Park to take up permanent residence in Malibu.

MALIBU TILES are distinguished by the rich color created by ceramicist Rufus B. Keeler and his artisans, who produced Mexican and Andalusian-style tiles at the Malibu Potteries from 1926 to 1932. In the six short years that the tiles of Malibu Potteries were in production, these beautiful tiles became collectors' pieces. The Potteries produced not only wall and floor tiles, but also a whole range of products for swimming pools, tables, fountains, murals and decorative walls. Two of the most outstanding illustrations of Malibu tile can be seen in the outdoor fountain and the Persian carpet pattern inlaid in the loggia of the Adamson house, both designed by artist William Edward Handley.

2

"*Driving over the hard sand by the side of the sea inhaling the life-giving ozone as we go along!*"

—FREDERICK HASTINGS RINDGE

is so exhilarating,

TOM MIX, the stylish cowboy star of silent films, poses in his Locomobile touring sedan on the road to Malibu. Circa 1920.

ARCH ROCK near Topanga may have added a scenic touch to the coastline, but for travelers, it was just another obstacle on the wagon trail to Malibu at the turn of the century. The trail from Santa Monica to the beginning of the Rindge Ranch could only be traveled at low tide.
In 1906 after a big storm, the rock disappeared, some say with a little help from dynamite.

Route 1, the Pacific Coast Highway, or "PCH," spans the coastline of Malibu and about fifty-three thousand cars travel to and through Malibu daily—as many as seventy-eight thousand in the summer months. While commuters will say that there's nothing better than a drive along the coast on a perfect Malibu day, they admit to a love-hate relationship with PCH.

It's difficult to imagine a time when there was no public road through Malibu, no road that connected Malibu to the rest of the world, or connected Santa Monica to points north. But indeed, that was the case.

When Frederick Rindge purchased the Malibu rancho in 1893 he cleared a wagon trail, a little road running through the ranch on the smooth sandy beach, that could only be traveled at low tide. It became known as "the beach road." He also erected locked gates, one at

CASTLE ROCK is no longer on Pacific Coast Highway, but it was located just below Villa Leon, the castle-like thirty-five-room residence built by Leon Kauffman and his wife in 1928 on Coastline Drive at PCH. The couple lived there only until 1935. The house remained empty until 1952, when it was sold at auction for seventy-one thousand dollars.

the eastern entrance to the ranch and the other at Malibu Canyon on the road that led to his home. He offered keys to homesteaders who lived in what are now known as Encinal and Decker canyons north of the Rindge ranch. They cleared wagon trails down to the beach, then used Rindge's beach trail through the ranch to get to Santa Monica. In 1905 Rindge established a substantial wagon road from the gate of the ranch to Malibu Canyon where his home was located, and posted "No Trespassing" signs along it. In 1907, two years after her husband's death, May Rindge built a fence across the beach road. By 1910 a public highway opened that stretched from the northern boundary of Santa Monica to the southern boundary of *Rancho Topanga Malibu Sequit*. May Rindge was determined to keep her land and her road private, but nearby homesteaders were just as determined to change that—

especially since May had guards at the Las Flores Canyon gate to her ranch.

Although May had fought her case to protect her private road all the way to the California Supreme Court and had won, the homesteaders and ranchers persisted, seeking support from nearby cities. In 1917 the city council of Santa Monica and a bevy of homesteaders, including C.M. Decker (whose family name would eventually be immortalized as a canyon), petitioned the Los Angeles County Board of Supervisors for public access through the Rindge property. Finally, in 1919 the county filed condemnation proceedings to make way for a public, two-lane dirt road through the ranch. After more than ten years of litigation, Malibu Road was completed, connecting the route from Las Flores Canyon to the Ventura County line, and opened to the public November 3, 1921. May continued to file appeals in an attempt to win back her private road, but the appeals were continually denied. Then, in a final blow in 1927, May Rindge's Marblehead Land Company was forced to deed land to the State of California, land that would be covered by a new highway.

The Roosevelt Highway was completed in 1929, making it possible for automobiles to travel along the coast from Santa Barbara to San Diego. The state widened the road to four lanes in 1947 and it became part of Route 1, the Pacific Coast Highway.

TOURING TOPICS was the magazine of the Automobile Club of Southern California. In 1910, Henry Keller (who had inherited the Malibu Ranch and sold it to Frederick H. Rindge in 1892) was a board member of the association and arranged a "club run" with a Spanish-style barbecue in a sycamore grove on the old ranch. Two hundred twenty-seven vehicles carried more than fifteen hundred guests who made the three-hour, one-way trip of thirty miles from 1st and Hill streets in Los Angeles. At the famous Malibu Run Barbecue, a twelve-piece orchestra played everything from opera to ragtime while the guests participated in games and races and the beef roasted in the pits. As *Touring Topics* noted, winners of the races (the sack race, fat man's race, fifty-yard dash) and the baseball games (the Four Cylinders played the Six Cylinders) were awarded prizes such as "bridge sets, fishing rods, a razor, manicure sets, pennants, a bathing suit and even a coffee loving cup!"

OPENING DAY of Roosevelt Highway was
June 29, 1929. In a ceremony at Little Sycamore
Canyon, north of Malibu, California's Governor
Charles C. Young cut the ribbon on the final link—
the road through the Malibu rancho—connecting the
coastal road from San Diego to Santa Barbara.

3

> "This coast offers inducements
> for the building of a
> road well-neigh **equal to**
> Italy's famous Cornice Road."
>
> —FREDERICK HASTINGS RINDGE

LAS FLORES, LA COSTA AND CARBON BEACHES

MALIBU'S OLD BRICK COURTHOUSE was designed by Butler and Butler and built in 1933 by Maurice Hirchfield. He leased the building to the county which used it to house the court presided over first by Judge John Webster, and then by Judge John Merrick until it closed in 1972. A jail cell and sheriffs' station were also in this building. On occasion, church services were held here, and the choir sat in the jury box.

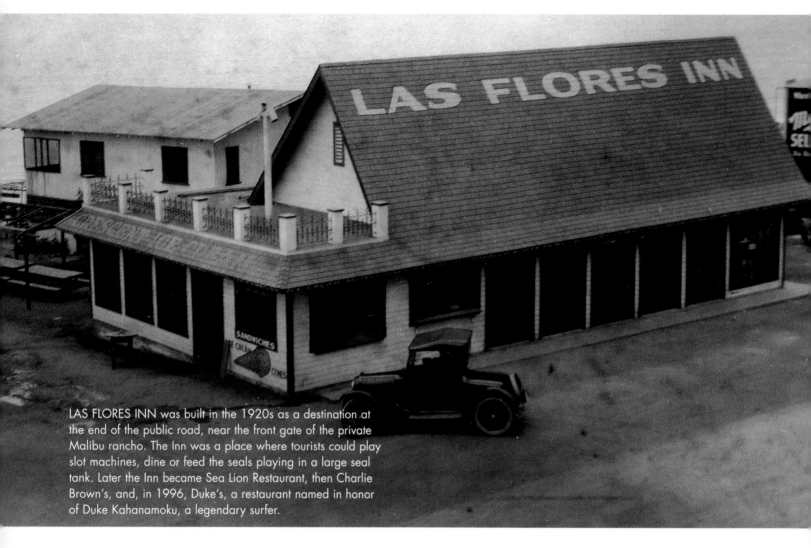

LAS FLORES INN was built in the 1920s as a destination at the end of the public road, near the front gate of the private Malibu rancho. The Inn was a place where tourists could play slot machines, dine or feed the seals playing in a large seal tank. Later the Inn became Sea Lion Restaurant, then Charlie Brown's, and, in 1996, Duke's, a restaurant named in honor of Duke Kahanamoku, a legendary surfer.

Until 1921, when the road was completed through the Rindge ranch, few people had seen the area north of Las Flores Canyon. Homesteaders built hunting cabins up Las Flores Canyon where deer, rabbits and quail were plentiful, but the area was still a mystery to the general public. Frederick Rindge had once envisioned Malibu to be like Europe's Riviera, with "coaching roads" where horse-drawn coaches would carry people along the hilltops surrounding La Costa and Carbon Canyon to see the grand views. Coaching roads remain only a dreamer's dream in Malibu, but nothing inhibits the magnificent vistas of Santa Monica Bay from modern-day Rambla Pacifico. The scenic road has been inaccessible since 1980 when landslides forced its closure.

Defeated in her attempts to maintain the privacy of her rancho and in need of cash to pay her mounting legal bills, May Rindge's Marblehead Land Company sold La Costa beachfront in 1926 to developer Harold

A MALIBU FIRESTORM burned over the ridge at Carbon Beach in the 1930s. Malibu is notorious for its disastrous fires which are most often caused by the dreaded, hot and dry Santa Ana winds that blow in Southern California from September through early December. History shows that fires plagued the Chumash in Malibu long before the area was highly populated, and these Native Americans controlled blazes using annual preventive burns. The earliest Malibu fire was recorded in *Two Years Before the Mast* by explorer Richard Henry Dana in 1835 when it was still Tapia property.

Ferguson for six million dollars. He subdivided the beach-front into about fifty-five parcels and developed the La Costa Beach Club for the land-side property owners. Ferguson sold a few parcels, but became entangled in a lawsuit that sent him to jail. Ownership of the property reverted to May Rindge. As president of Marblehead Land Company, she floated a six-million-dollar bond in 1928 for improvements to develop the Malibu ranch, but the value of the bonds dropped to ten cents on the dollar when the stock market crashed the next year.

In 1927 Art Jones opened Malibu's first realty office, with the sole purpose of leasing the Malibu Colony property for the Marblehead Land Company. Jones also built the Malibu Inn adjoining his office, which was one of the first commercial buildings in Malibu. David Duncan joined Art Jones Realty in 1930 to direct the sales of La Costa Beach and Carbon Beach.

LITTLE HAS CHANGED except the look of the automobiles at the first commercial property in Malibu. Built in the 1940s at La Costa on PCH between Las Flores and Rambla Pacifico, it housed Sales Market (which eventually became A&B Plumbing), one of the few places to get supplies in the area. By the mid-Forties, Malibu had enough year-round residents to require a post office (Malibu residents picked up their mail at the Las Flores Post Office until the early 1950s).

MALIBU RANCHO FOR SALE. IN 1940, the entire Malibu rancho was put up for sale. The senior Louis T. Busch, who had worked on the subdivision of land with the Marblehead Land Company, opened a sales office on Malibu Road. In December 1940, he advertised in the *Santa Monica Outlook*: "17,000 acres and 22 miles of beach of the Malibu Ranch is to be broken up and sold. Beach bungalows on the beach for $6,000 to $9,000; 442 acres for a hotel and club site, $98.50 an acre; a fine sandy 1000-foot beach lot, $15,000; a motel site of 6 acres with 900 feet of private beach, $12,000; and 100 to 640 acre ranches for $100 an acre." In 1946, a year after his father's death, Louis T. Busch, Jr.— fresh out of the Navy—opened his own office on Malibu Road. He built the Pacific Coast Highway office photographed here in the mid-Sixties. Busch, Bob Stroms, Tom Doyle and few other local Realtors sold all of Malibu's virgin land.

THE MYSTERIOUS ALBATROSS was on the beachfront at Las Flores Canyon. The proprietor Mrs. Burnett was a true Malibu character with a salty tongue. She bought the property in 1941 and built the Albatross, a hotel and restaurant that locals called a hideaway for illicit lovers. After the war, Mrs. Burnett bought some searchlights and put one on the top of the Albatross where it would sweep around, flashing light into all the surrounding area. The neighbors complained, so Judge John Merrick (who presided in the courthouse across the street) and Reeves Templeton (who was then the publisher of the *Malibu Times* and lived in the neighborhood) paid her a visit and convinced her to keep the searchlight stationary. The Albatross was abandoned and burned to the ground in the early 1970s. All that's left of the Albatross are this matchbook cover and a few scenes in the 1960 Warner Brothers film *Strangers When We Meet*, starring Kirk Douglas and Kim Novak.

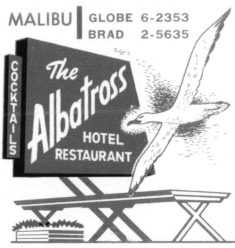

MALIBU | GLOBE 6-2353
BRAD 2-5635

COCKTAILS

The Albatross
HOTEL RESTAURANT

21202 W. PACIFIC COAST HWY.

MALIBU VINEYARDS. Michael and Kim McCarty rebuilt their art-filled family home after the fire in 1993, and planted a vineyard, which surrounds the property in the La Costa hills and serves as a fire break. Their wine is bottled under the label Malibu Vineyards. Michael McCarty is the proprietor of the renowned Michael's restaurants in Santa Monica and New York.

LAS FLORES CANYON

Las Flores Canyon Road

La Costa Beach Club

Duke's Restaurant

CARBON/DEAL BEACH. Carbon Beach has become known as Deal Beach since it is home to many of the richest people in America, including such notables as Eli Broad, David Geffen, former Los Angeles mayor Richard Riordan, Terry Semel, Jeffery Katzenberg and Haim Saban. Software billionaire Larry Ellison upped the ante for property on Deal Beach in 2003 when he bought five forty-foot properties for sixty-five million dollars. Most of the homes on Carbon/Deal Beach are contemporary architectural statements in sharp contrast to the Thirties beach house shown above. Many original Carbon Beach houses have been torn down and replaced by homes designed by internationally renowned architects such as Michael Graves, John Lautner and Richard Meier.

MALIBU MODERN.
Richard Meier, the
architect responsible for
The Getty Center in
Brentwood, designed
this light-infused 4,280
square foot beach
residence on two lots
at Carbon Beach.

AQUARIUS, a sport-fishing boat, arrived at the Malibu Pier in the Seventies and operated until the pier closed in 1994. The State Parks Department spent ten years stabilizing and restoring the pier to the original look it had in 1950. Plans for the restored pier feature a charter boat, a whale-watching boat (in season), a bait-and-tackle shop, a café, an office and mooring for a Los Angeles County lifeguard rescue boat, a surf museum, an art gallery in the towers at the tip of the pier and a restaurant at the site of the legendary Alice's Restaurant.

MALIBU PIER. When the Rindges' Marblehead Land Company declared bankruptcy in 1936, its Malibu pier was taken over by bondholders who had helped fund the real estate development of the ranch. When war was looming in 1941, the U.S. Coast Guard used the pier. In 1944, it was sold for fifty thousand dollars to William Huber with the condition that he construct a building to house the Coast Guard for the duration of the war, but the war ended before the building was complete. He improved the pier and built the twin towers for a bait-and-tackle shop in the south tower and a café in the north tower.

The sport-fishing boats *Lindbrook* and *Scooby-Do* operated off the Malibu Pier in the Forties until the early Sixties. Huber originally leased the Coast Guard building to Henry Guttman for the Malibu Sports Club Restaurant in 1966. A few years later with new owners, Al Carter and Ron McClain, the eatery was renamed the Malibu Pier Club. Finally it became Alice's Restaurant in 1972, a tourist favorite until the pier closed in 1994. The state purchased the pier in 1980, but it was severely damaged by El Niño storms in 1983 and was closed for a couple of years. It reopened and became a California Point of Interest, but it had to close again because of heavy storms in 1994.

4

"How many and varied

are the **moods of the sea!**

It has a mood to fit every mood of man."

—FREDERICK HASTINGS RINDGE

In the Twenties and Thirties, Malibu Beach was a lure for surfers. Pioneers to the sport would crawl through the fence at the Malibu Potteries factory and paddle the mile up to what is now called Surfrider Beach. Situated on a point, Surfrider is a south-facing beach with a very well-shaped curl and a long ride. At the end of September waves have been known to reach eight to ten feet. By the late Fifties, the film *Gidget* (1959) starring Sandra Dee and James Darren as "Moondoggie," turned Surfrider and Malibu surf culture into a mainstream-USA phenomenon. If *Gidget* didn't convince everybody that they wanted to be surfers, the Beach Boys did with their string of 1960s surf-song hits.

California was first introduced to surfing in 1907, when Henry Huntington (president of the Southern Pacific Railroad) hired Hawaiian George Freeth to demonstrate the sport when he opened the new Southern Pacific rail service connecting Los Angeles and Redondo Beach. But it wasn't until fifteen years later that the sport caught on, when champion Olympic swimmer Duke Kahanamoku from Waikiki Beach taught surfing in Santa Monica. The charismatic Duke, the ambassador of surfing who went on to make seventeen Hollywood films, was a lifeguard at The Beach Club in Santa Monica. Tom Blake was lifeguard at The Swim Club, which was next door to the north of The Beach Club. Blake built his own surfboards and had perfected the hollow board in 1926 while in Hawaii. While living in Santa Monica, Blake worked with Thomas N. Rogers in Venice to manufacture the hollow board that transformed the sport. These legendary surfers and lifeguards would become pioneers of surfing and the sport would become part of the way of life in Malibu.

In the 1950s Malibu was Mecca for surfers, and many of the locals became legends beyond their familiar sand. Mickey "Mongoose" Munoz, Matt Kivlin, Mickey Dora and Johnny Fain got their first brush with fame in Hollywood films such as *Gidget*, in which Fain donned a wig and bikini as Sandra Dee's stand-in for the surfing scenes and the others performed on the waves. Although local surfers were disgusted by the romanticized and silly beach love stories, they didn't turn down the opportunity

THE MALIBU SUNSET outlines Malibu surf points, Surfrider in the foreground and Point Dume in the distance.

to appear in the films. In fact, the four who surfed in *Gidget* went on to ride the waves in the next ten beach-surf films that followed in the Sixties. Soon wannabes far from any ocean became devotees. Surfing was portrayed as the California dream come true.

Malibu local and longboard designer Lance Carson recalls the early Malibu Beach surf scene when "You could surf every wave you wanted. All the people would sit around the wall at Malibu Beach—which we would call 'The Pit.' We would play ukuleles, wear cut-off jeans and straw hats and drink beer as we watched Dale Velzy shape boards. " But with all the attention focused on surfing and Malibu, those surf-any-wave days were numbered. Many left Malibu in search of bigger waves and fewer crowds. But their hearts, and the tradition they initiated, belonged to Malibu.

THE WALL surrounded the Adamson House and its vast gardens, but it also defined the entrance to Surfrider Beach. The unique, decorative wall constructed of boulders, tiles and cement covered the property at Vaquero Point and continued south to the pier. This part was removed in 1968 when the California State Parks Department acquired Surfrider.

THE REAL GIDGET, Kathy Kohner, stands at the "shack" on Malibu Beach in 1956. Based on her Fifties diaries about her adventures learning to surf and hanging out with the cast of male surfers, her father Frederick Kohner wrote a spiced-up novel, *Gidget*. Actually, there were very few girls surfing in the Fifties. Kathy snapped photos of these surfers, such as Jerry Hurst, Terry-Michael Tracy, Les Arndt, artist "Moondoggie" Billy Al Bengston and Bill Jensen at Surfrider in 1956 to 1957, before the film *Gidget* hit American screens in 1959. This snapshot is from Kathy Kohner's personal collection.

Eventually co-ed surf camps, lighter boards and wetsuits made surfing an appealing sport for girls. International women's competitions and surfing magazines may all owe their origins to the early fascination with the real Gidget of Malibu.

BIG WAVE RIDER Laird Hamilton is one of the most respected and photographed athletes in crossover board sports in the world. He has taken extreme sports such as tow-in big wave riding, kite surfing, air-boarding, jet ski surfing, rock climbing, mountain biking, ocean paddle-boarding and snowboarding to new heights with his daring approaches. Hamilton designs, makes and tests new gear, such as the hydrofoil surf ski, to improve the skill in these sports. Laird has been featured in many documentary surf films on tow-in big wave surfing. He and his film crew advise and furnish surfers for other film companies, as well as shoot their own movies. He and his wife Gabrielle Reece reside in Malibu and Hawaii.

Malibu

THE MARLBORO MAN. Jefferson Wagner, a local Malibu surfer was a male model who became known internationally as "The Marlboro Man" from 1986 to 1991. The most visible of the Malibu Pier Partners (the concessionaires of the pier), Jay oversees the daily operation of the pier. Zuma Jay, his surf shop, sells and rents surf gear in Malibu, but he still finds time to assist with coaching the Malibu High surfing team.

SURF MUSIC brought Malibu into homes around the world. Its pioneers included Dick Dale and the Del-Tones, Jan and Dean and the Surfaris, but it was the Beach Boys on Capitol Records who took the genre to commercial heights. With its cover photographed at Malibu's Paradise Cove, the first Beach Boys album—*Surfin' Safari*—made its debut in 1962. Before long, hodaddies all over the world knew the words and were humming the tunes.

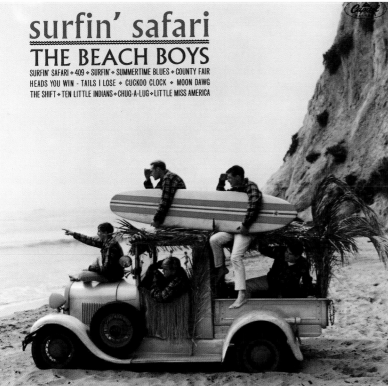

"KITESURFING is the next swell in the thrill rides—faster, longer, higher," wrote Roy M. Wallack in the *Los Angeles Times*. "Kite-boarders, the extreme of the board adventurers, are inventing all kinds of aerial maneuvers." Malibu kite-surfer Jamie Padgett, who keeps a wardrobe of kites and boards for different wind velocities and different waves, describes his sport as a combination of wake-boarding, sailing, doing tricks and flying. When Malibu's onshore winds start to blow twenty to thirty knots, kite-surfers head for Leo Carrillo and County Line beaches.

PAPA JACK'S. Surfing is the granddaddy of all extreme sports. Now surfing on wheels is labeled an extreme sport with fans all over the world. Papa Jack's Skate Park in Malibu has a professionally designed all-steel street course and offers a summer camp. Thomas Skene is shown here riding one of the eight-foot ramps in this ten-thousand-square-foot skating space.

MALIBU MAKOS KIDS' SUMMER SURF CAMP is held every summer at Zuma Beach (and in Australia when winter comes to Malibu). The boogie-board campers are taught by trained water-sports experts and lifeguards who focus on conditioning, water safety, surfing and kayaking.

Serra Retreat

Malibu Creek

Serra Retreat Road

Malibu Inn

Surfrider Beach

Adamson House

Malibu Pier

MALIBU PIER AND SERRA RETREAT

5

MALIBU LAGOON

"*Happy* is the man to whom
Nature has not lost its charm."

—Frederick Hastings Rindge

MALIBU LAGOON, a bird sanctuary,
is a resting place for the seagulls, pelicans,
mallard and canvasback ducks, coots,
white egrets, sea pigeons and ibis.

alibu Creek flows through Malibu Canyon, the only one of Malibu's thirteen canyons whose water flows from the San Fernando Valley through the majestic Santa Monica Mountains to the Pacific Ocean. Over time a berm has formed that directs the creek's gentle waters to the sea. At that very spot, a beautiful lagoon that formed has become a peaceful resting spot for thousands of migrating birds. The natural

avian sanctuary at the mouth of Malibu Creek was a peaceful vista for the Chumash, whose Humaliwo village was situated just south of the lagoon at Vaquero Point. Archaeologists have dated remnants of the village back to the 1400s. The setting was not just beautiful, but practical, too, a spot where the villagers could find fresh water from the creek, a calm beach to launch their canoes and a nearby canyon ripe for hunting and gathering.

SERRA RETREAT. In 1942, little more than a year after May Rindge died, her unfinished castle situated on Laudamus Hill was purchased for fifty thousand dollars by the Franciscan Order of California. The Franciscans finished it, as shown in this 1949 image, but most of its classic Malibu tiles were lost when the building was destroyed by fire in 1970. Still lived in and maintained by the friars, Serra Retreat has a commanding 360-degree view and is open to groups seeking "renewal of the spirit."

Years later, in 1929, Rhoda Rindge, the daughter of Frederick and May Rindge, and her husband Merritt Adamson commissioned architect Stiles Clements to design their magnificent Adamson House (now known as the Malibu Lagoon Museum) at the same location where the Chumash had once lived. The home is a testament to the beauty of the tiles created by May Rindge's Malibu Potteries, a factory established in 1926 on a site two miles west of Las Flores Canyon and about one-half mile east of Malibu Pier, spanning fifteen hundred feet of beach frontage. In the hills above, May Rindge started building her dream house, a fifty-room manse that would eventually become the home to Franciscan padres. Known as Serra Retreat, it soon became the centerpiece of Malibu.

THE CASTLE overlooking Malibu was built in 1982 by Tom Hodges, M.D. His travels in Europe inspired him to design and build this fortress-castle. The Castle is now owned by philanthropist Lilly Lawrence, who generously opens her castle to support the Malibu community and its nonprofit organizations.

SCHOOL WITH A VIEW. George Pepperdine founded Pepperdine University in 1937. The Adamson family donated one hundred thirty-eight acres to Pepperdine in 1968 and the campus opened in the fall of 1972. Pepperdine acquired more land, and today the Malibu campus is beautifully situated on eight hundred thirty acres. The university has approximately five thousand students enrolled in the under-graduate liberal arts school Seaver College and three graduate schools: the Pepperdine School of Law, the Graziadio School of Business and Management and its newest, the Pepperdine University School of Public Policy. The 1984 Olympic water polo competition was held at Pepperdine. Despite its location at Malibu Canyon Road and Pacific Coast Highway, Pepperdine is outside Malibu city limits.

"To receive the strength of the mountains,

by dwelling in their company—

this is living!"

—FREDERICK HASTINGS RINDGE

Malibu Canyon has been a hunting ground since the days of the Chumash. And for more than a century, nature has been at the mercy of those men with weapons. When brothers John and Ron Rindge were researching the history of their ancestors' land, they discovered the story of "Mountain Man" Andrew Sublette. Sublette was on a bear-hunting trip in lower Malibu Canyon on December 17, 1853, when he encountered two grizzly bears. The Rindges wrote, "After killing one of the bears and while in the process of reloading his rifle, Andy was set upon by the other enraged bear. Andy, with his hunting knife, aided by his dog, Old Buck, overcame the second bear, but was terribly mauled in this battle of man and beast. A nearby hunting companion, aided by *vaqueros* from the Malibu valley plains below the canyon, took Andy to Los Angeles, where he succumbed

the next day. His faithful dog, Old Buck, died three days later from the trauma of losing his master."

The canyon provided a respite for travelers and for those looking for a way to escape the pressures of the city. In 1910, a homesteader built a cabin on Piuma Road and two decades later that cabin became known as Crater Camp, a summer resort. In 1947 the cabin was moved up the road and established as the Saddle Peak Lodge, a restaurant that quickly became popular with the movie industry set, despite its isolated location in the middle of the Santa Monica Mountains. Stars and film crews on location at the nearby Paramount Ranch and 20th Century Fox Ranch discovered it.

Malibu competitive surfer Johnny Fain fondly recalls growing up in Malibu and playing in the canyon, "We would go up Malibu Creek and catch catfish, trout

and bass. There were different swimming holes to explore all the way up to the dam. The water was crystal clear. You could put your head under a rock waterfall and drink the cool spring water."

The early large ranch properties up Malibu Canyon Road, past the Malibu dam and through the Malibu tunnel, now belong to the National Park Service and California State Parks. These include Malibu State Park (which includes the first ranch owned by the fortieth president of the United States, Ronald Reagan), the Peter Strauss Ranch (named for the actor who once owned the property), and the Paramount Ranch, where movies and television programs have been filmed for years. And in the center of the Santa Monica Mountains, the vineyards of Rosenthal-The Malibu Estate, Semler and Jussila cover the mountainsides.

MALIBU STATE PARK is situated near spectacular rugged mountains and Malibu Creek. In 1901 it was the site of the Crags Country Club, formed by businessmen, which flourished until the Depression hit in the early Thirties. Membership declined and the club closed. After 20th Century Fox filmed *How Green Was My Valley* here in 1941, the studio bought the property and filmed many movies on the land. In 1974 the State of California purchased the Crags Country Club property as well as the adjoining Reagan and Hope ranches. These ten thousand acres became Malibu State Park. The park has thirty miles of hiking trails, including part of the famed Backbone Trail.

THE PINK LADY. On October 28, 1966, a mysterious sixty-foot naked lady appeared on the rocks over the Malibu Canyon tunnel. No one seemed to notice how she got there—or they just chose to ignore her gradual arrival. Some called her obscene and the county called her a traffic hazard, but for Malibuites she was *The Pink Lady*. Although she received headlines and televison coverage during her short stay, she was covered by brown paint six days after she appeared.

Artist Lynne Westmore Seemayer, who traveled the canyon to visit her mother, was inspired to paint a bird to cover the graffiti on the canyon rocks. Several nights a week for several months, the artist scaled the rocks, supporting herself with nylon ropes. After removing the graffiti, she spent two months drawing an outline, which emerged as a female form rather than a bird. Finally, on the night of the full moon, Seemayer completed her "masterpiece," the sixty-foot naked lady holding a bouquet of pink flowers. In the lower left of the photograph, a *Los Angeles Times* photographer takes a picture of the artist and *The Pink Lady*.

STRAUSS RANCH. An original coast live oak, dating to 1881, still flourishes on the Peter Strauss Ranch woodland on Triunfo Creek where the Chumash once resided. In 1900, Harry Miller purchased the property as a weekend retreat and built a stone house and lookout tower, but lost the property in the Depression. Arthur Edeson and Warren Shobert purchased the ranch in 1935, improving it to become an amusement park for swimming and boating, which they called Shosan. When they built a dam on Triunfo Creek, the property became known as Lake Enchanto. Competition from other resorts led to closure in 1960. Actor Peter Strauss, on location during the filming of *Rich Man, Poor Man* at Malibu Lake in 1976, bought this beautiful woodland, restored it to its original state and resided there until 1983. He sold it to the Santa Monica Mountains Conservancy, which transferred it to the National Park Service in 1987.

PARAMOUNT RANCH. Paramount purchased twenty-four hundred acres of *Rancho Las Virgenes* in 1927 for its movie ranch, the perfect setting for the golden age of Hollywood westerns. When that era ended, Paramount sold the ranch to western fan William Hertz in 1953. He built an Old West town and promoted filming on the property. He, in turn, sold in 1955. The Paramount Racetrack opened for a year, but the ranch continued to change ownership until 1980, when the National Park Service purchased it. Paramount Ranch continues as a prime film location. Western films such as *Wagon Wheels* (1934) and *Klondike Annie* (1936) and later television series such as *Gunsmoke* (1955–1975), *The Cisco Kid* (1950–1956) and *Dr. Quinn, Medicine Woman* (1993–1998), which starred Malibu resident Jane Seymour, were filmed here. The park's trails are named for film productions shot on location at the ranch. Visit the old western town, hike the trails and, if one is lucky, even watch a film being made or hear the music of the Topanga Banjo Fiddle Contest held here every May.

MALIBU WINERIES. Malibu's history of vineyards dates back to 1802 when José Bartolomé Tapia, one of the first Mexican settlers, planted vines. Leon Victor Prudhomme, the Frenchman who married Tapia's granddaughter, was very interested in winemaking and Don Mateo Keller was a vintner in Los Angeles. Because the rancho's next owner Frederick Rindge was a supporter of the temperance movement, he put a stop to growing wine grapes in Malibu by the turn of the twentieth century. A hundred years later, however, vineyards are being cultivated in the center of the Santa Monica Mountains and along the Malibu coast. The Malibu Wine Association has twenty members, many of whom pick and press their grapes and send the juice to be processed, aged and bottled at wineries on the central coast and in the Santa Inez Valley north of Santa Barbara. The pioneer Malibu vintner is

entrepreneur George Rosenthal, who bought twenty-five acres in upper Newton Canyon in 1987, planted a vineyard and expanded to two hundred forty acres. Rosenthal's wines have received excellent reviews.

Semler Saddle Rock Ranch is situated between two spectacular rock formations, Turtle Rock and Saddle Rock, in the heart of the Santa Monica Mountains. It is a picturesque working ranch, consisting of almost a thousand acres of green meadows, a natural lake, hillsides planted in avocado trees and wine grape vineyards, with horses and exotic animals grazing peacefully in the meadows. Ronnie Semler bought this property after the 1979 fire and became its third owner since the Spanish land grants. The Chumash inhabited this site, as many artifacts and well-protected cave pictographs dating to around 1780 attest.

7

THE MALIBU COLONY

"To lose one's self

by the side of the sea!"

—FREDERICK HASTINGS RINDGE

COLONY COTTAGES. Sara Hamilton wrote in the fan magazine *Photoplay* dated September 1932: "Mad, Merry Malibu. The cradle of the beach pajama and the home of the five-thousand-dollar-a-week beachcomber. The most interesting and the goofiest stretch of sand in the world, where the antics of the stars make the seagulls dizzy. A half-mile stretch of delirium tremens architecture along an astounded Pacific Ocean. A place where the stars go, 'to get away from it all,' but build their houses with a tiny three feet between. Every house screaming out the personality of the owner, a dead giveaway. Even the fish can't get over it, while the seagulls fly dizzily around, squawking for help and a bit more caviar."

THE COLONY 1940. The larger house and tennis courts were built after the land was sold rather than leased.

In 1926 May Rindge developed the Malibu Beach Motion Picture Colony, located on the beach just north of Malibu Creek. When film star Anna Q. Nilsson built her beach cottage in Malibu Colony, as it has come to be known, it was the first time that *Rancho Malibu* went public. These thirty-foot-wide beachfront lots were leased for ten years at a dollar per foot per month, but the desirability of living at The Colony caused the Rindges' Marblehead Land Company to rethink the entire property. The company further subdivided and sold off the land that had once been Frederick Rindge's beloved *Rancho Malibu*.

Following Nilsson's lead, many film stars leased the property and built summer beach cottages. Among the first notable lessors were Bing Crosby and Ronald Colman (who were both fishermen), Marie Dressler, Warner Baxter, Gary Cooper, Gloria Swanson, Harold Lloyd, Constance Bennett, John Gilbert, Lilyan Tashman and Jackie Coogan. With its gated and guarded entrance to assure privacy, The Colony properties started Hollywood's romance with Malibu. The celebrities shared a devotion to the isolation of this little paradise a mere twenty miles from Hollywood.

When the leases ran out in 1936, the land was offered for sale. Most of the cottages were razed or remodeled into larger structures. After World War II, a new cast of stars took up residence in The Colony, including

Malibu

MALIBU INN. In the 1930s, the Malibu Inn on Malibu Road provided the only local entertainment—a jukebox and pinball machine. The locals could get a Coke at the fountain or pick up a card game in the back room. When the road was rerouted up the hill, the Malibu Inn was relocated to its permanent spot, across from the Malibu Pier.

Burgess Meredith, Cary Grant and Betsy Drake, Brian Donlevy and June Lockhart.

During the Forties and Fifties social life bloomed on the tennis courts, with a tennis tournament every summer. A tennis court was the stage for the Malibu Colony Little Theatre, where Robert Walker and Warner Baxter would round up The Colony talent and present productions during the last weekends of summer.

The Fifties brought Lana Turner (her mother lived in Escondido Canyon). Then in the Seventies and Eighties the parade of stars began. Dyan Cannon, Lee Majors and later tennis player Robert Redford (during the filming of *The Sting* with Paul Newman), Larry Hagman (who always flew the flag when he was home), Rod Steiger (in residence thirty-two years), Lee Marvin, Roman Polanski, Sharon Tate and Linda Ronstadt (whose love affair with then-governor Jerry Brown helped ban three-wheeled all-terrain vehicles on PCH through Malibu). Malibu has become the address for many celebrities—some vacationing, others living year-round. Unlike the days when stars lived only in The Colony, today their addresses are scattered from the hills to Carbon Beach, Point Dume, Paradise Cove, Broad Beach and Encinal Beach. In the words of Arnold York, publisher of *Malibu Times,* "Ask any celebrity: one of the things they like best about Malibu is that they are left alone here."

ANNA Q. NILSSON, the glamorous Swedish silent film star, poses in front of her colony beach cottage with journalist Gladys Hall, right. Seeking a place out of the limelight, the model-turned-actress was one of the first to lease land and build a summer cottage in Malibu. Born in 1890, she made her first silent film in 1911, starred in such silent classics as *Adam's Rib* (1923) and *Vanity's Price* (1924), but when "talkies" came in, her heavy Swedish accent worked against her. She made a cameo appearance in *Sunset Boulevard* (1950) and died in 1974.

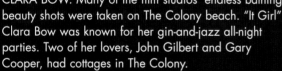

CLARA BOW. Many of the film studios' endless bathing beauty shots were taken on The Colony beach. "It Girl" Clara Bow was known for her gin-and-jazz all-night parties. Two of her lovers, John Gilbert and Gary Cooper, had cottages in The Colony.

DOLORES DEL RIO. Another early Colony resident, Dolores Del Rio became one of Hollywoods' biggest stars, renowned for her exquisite beauty and incredible style. After she became a star, she married the renowned MGM production designer Cedric Gibbons. When they divorced, she had a much-publicized affair with Orson Welles.

CONSTANCE BENNETT.
Sophisticated comedic actress of the Thirties Constance Bennett relaxes at her Malibu Colony house.

WARNER BAXTER.
Longtime Malibu Colony residents Warner Baxter and wife Winifred Bryson have fun on The Colony beach.

A BEACH PARTY in The Colony in 1931 was the focus of photographer Edward Steichen. Silent-film actress Lilyan Tashman was the hostess and among her guests were Eddie Lowe, Joan Crawford and Douglas Fairbanks, Jr.

MALIBU AND THE COLONY

HRL Laboratories

Malibu Canyon Road

Malibu Tennis Club

Los Angeles County Complex

Malibu Plaza

Pacific Coast Highway

The Colony

Serra Retreat

Malibu Creek

Malibu Country Mart

Malibu Creek Plaza

Malibu Creek Bridge

o Golf Course

THE COLONY 2004. Just as in the Golden Age of Hollywood, Malibu and The Colony are a huge draw for the privacy-craving celebrity set.

Pepperdine Tennis Courts

Pacific Coast Highway

Malibu Canyon Road

Bluffs Park

Old Malibu Road

MALIBU ROAD

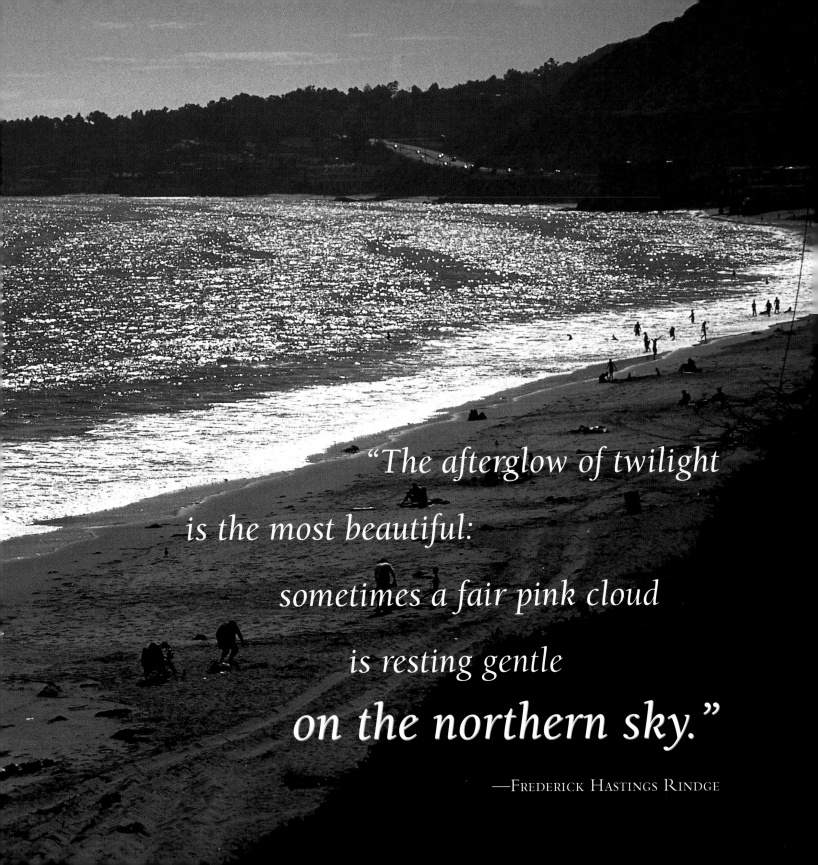

8

"The afterglow of twilight

is the most beautiful:

sometimes a fair pink cloud

is resting gentle

on the northern sky."

—FREDERICK HASTINGS RINDGE

MALIBU'S OLDEST BUILDING has a remarkable history. After the Homestead Act in 1880, homesteaders and squatters began to settle in the Santa Monica Mountains. The Swinney family built a cabin in Solstice Canyon, but later it was found to overstep the boundary of the rancho, so it was moved. In 1899, after he sold Malibu rancho, Henry Keller bought the Swinney property, but the fire of 1903 destroyed the wood cabin—the same fire that burned the Rindge house in Malibu Canyon. In 1904, Keller rebuilt a house of stone from the creek on exactly the same site, and it still stands. This is probably the oldest building left in Malibu, in the same area in which the Chumash hunted and found shelter.

Once called "Coral Beach" by Frederick Hastings Rindge, the modern-day Corral Beach is one of Malibu's most photographed spots. Traveling north up Pacific Coast Highway, passers-by can see nuances of change each day in this area, depending on the weather and the light—rainbows, glowing sunsets, swirling fog—and if they look back to the road just traveled, they see the stunning view of Santa Monica Bay.

Before the county bought Corral Beach in 1951, Walter Madge had a café and fishing camp resort on the beach. The rock star Cher built a palm-tree oasis that perches on the perfect point above this crescent beach, providing her a view of all Santa Monica Bay.

Across the highway at the bottom of Corral Canyon is the narrow entrance to Solstice Canyon, a favorite hunting ground and shelter for the Chumash, who called it Sostern or Sostomo Canyon. The creek here is fast-running and spills down rocky waterfalls canopied in old trees. Cattle, first brought by the Tapia family in 1802, graze in grand meadows. In this lovely canyon, Malibu's oldest building, the Keller House, was built in 1906 and sits above the rushing creek. Up the canyon are the remains of the Roberts' house, designed by Paul Williams, which was destroyed in the fire of 1982.

Up Corral Canyon are the spectacular rock formations of Castro Crest, and here the Backbone Trail

ROBERTS HOUSE. In the 1930s merchant Fred Roberts and his wife Florence, began buying property and water rights in Solstice Canyon. Roberts envisioned the canyon as a park. They built a house, designed by architect Paul Williams, which blended with the natural surroundings on a tropical terrace of lush trees and ferns bordered by a brook. Featured in *Architectural Digest* in 1954, the house unfortunately was destroyed in 1982 by fire, and the property was sold to the Santa Monica Conservancy. In the late 1980s, the land transferred to the National Park Service and finally is the public park Fred Roberts dreamed it would be.

intersects a dead-end road, a favorite of mountain bikers and hardy hikers. In the spring and summer, visitors are awed by Malibu's coastal slopes, alive with dazzling yellow mustard, coastal daisies and Scotch Broom.

Farther up Pacific Coast Highway near Latigo Point—which was originally called Rattlesnake Point, for good reason—the Rindge beach house stood until it was destroyed by high surf in the 1983 storm.

Marblehead Land Company opened the land between Escondido Canyon and the next canyon north, Ramirez, as a tract for sale in 1941, but World War II slowed sales considerably. The Ramirez Canyon land was leased as farmland to Al Thorpe. The end of this beautiful canyon, with its lush sycamore glade, houses an enclave of four homes on 22.5 acres formerly owned by Barbra Streisand. Streisand donated the land to the State of California, which dedicated the houses as offices for the Santa Monica Mountains Conservancy.

After the Malibu Pier closed in 1940, Captain Frank Wilson and Al Camp purchased picturesque Ramirez Canyon Beach and forty accompanying acres, planning to build a trailer park. But again, the war precluded obtaining sufficient building supplies, so they sold the property to the genial Bill Swanson in 1945. Swanson built a five-hundred-fifty-foot sports fishing pier, gatehouse, and a long-planned trailer park.

CORRAL CANYON intersects the Backbone Trail, which winds south through Topanga to Will Rogers Park in Pacific Palisades and north to Point Mugu State Park.

Backbone Trail
Corral Canyon Trailhead
Latigo Trailhead 4.2 mi.

AN OSCAR-WINNING PERFORMANCE. Joan Crawford in *Mildred Pierce* (1945), was directed by Michael Curtiz, who selected the Rindge house at Latigo Beach as an exterior setting. The house was destroyed by high surf in 1983.

OCEAN VIEW APARTMENTS

OCEAN VIEW APARTMENTS

CAR PARKING AREA

160
155
150
145
140
135
130

0 5 10 15 20 25 FEET

RESTAURANT   POOL

BEACH

Malibu

A SMALL HOTEL WITH A GRANDSTAND VIEW, Holiday House was built in 1948 by film director Dudley Murphy, who directed *Emperor Jones*, released in 1933. Richard Neutra designed this simple contemporary hotel for the steep site. All rooms had fireplaces, kitchens, and unobstructed ocean views with a terrace and glass-front walls to ensure privacy.

HOLIDAY HOUSE is the site of Geoffrey's Restaurant. The original Holiday House was a favorite hideaway for the film industry. The upper apartments have become condominiums.

RAMIREZ CANYON BEACH, NOW PARADISE COVE. "Paradise Cove, justly named, has gained fame as a trailerite's deluxe paradise," according to the Malibu Chamber of Commerce in 1952.

BANNING HARBOR was named
for Captain Phineas Banning.

"To this anchorage old Captain Phineas Banning used to come to load
his vessels with oak wood from the cañon (Ramirez Cañon) to be
taken to San Pedro. The oaks were topped for firewood, and in the
interim have regained their growth. This bay is sometimes known as
Banning Harbor."

—FREDERICK HASTINGS RINDGE

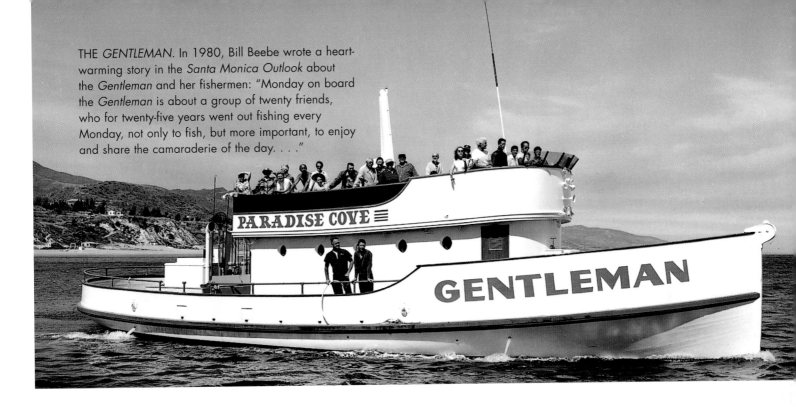

THE *GENTLEMAN*. In 1980, Bill Beebe wrote a heartwarming story in the *Santa Monica Outlook* about the *Gentleman* and her fishermen: "Monday on board the *Gentleman* is about a group of twenty friends, who for twenty-five years went out fishing every Monday, not only to fish, but more important, to enjoy and share the camaraderie of the day. . . ."

A DETECTIVE COMES TO THE COVE. While filming *The Rockford Files*, a popular television series in the 1970s, star James Garner used this trailer as both home and office. Garner played Jim Rockford and Noah Berry played his father. The show enjoyed a six-year run and was always filmed at Paradise Cove.

PARADISE DISCOVERED. The Morris family made Paradise Cove a true paradise for fisherman. After buying adjoining property from Fred Roberts for thirty-five hundred dollars an acre, the Morrises then bought the Swanson land along with its pier and restaurant—eventually creating a combined property of seventy acres. The Cove was a great attraction for fishermen and divers, with rental boats, a launch, a barge, and live-bait day boats, including the *Gentleman* and the *Betty-O*. The kelp beds attracted halibut, sea bass and yellowtail. Divers found more than enough lobster and abalone. In the early 1960s, the Cove was sold to Harry Kissel and is still owned and operated by his family. The end of the pier was destroyed in the 1983 storm. The *Gentleman* is long gone, along with the plentiful fish. Restaurateur Bob Morris has returned to the Cove and operates the Paradise Cove Beach Café.

IN A LEAFY GLADE is a lush, park-like setting of Sycamore trees at the end of Ramirez Canyon housing the offices of the Santa Monica Mountains Conservancy, a nonprofit state agency. It was established in 1980 by the California State Legislature to educate, own and manage parkland in Southern California. The Conservancy's mission statement reads: "Through direct action, alliances, partnerships, and joint powers authorities, the Conservancy's mission is to strategically buy back, preserve, protect, restore and enhance treasured pieces of Southern California to form an interlinking system of urban, rural, and river parks, open space, trails and wildlife habitats that are easily accessible to the general public."

In 1993, Barbra Streisand donated her ranch and four houses in Ramirez Canyon to the State of California. She and former husband Jon Peters originally bought a small stucco home on eight acres in 1974, converting it into a charming wood barn, with high ceilings and plenty of glass as a portal to the lovely natural surroundings. The "Barn" is now used as a Conservancy office and is rented for special functions. Over a period of five years in the 1970s, Streisand acquired the surrounding sixteen acres with four structures. The stable was transformed into a two-story Mediterranean villa guest house labeled "Peach House." The adjacent house took five years to convert into an authentic 1920s Art Deco house, which is frequently used as a location for films and photography.

THE BARN was originally a small stucco home.

BARWOOD is a post-and-beam Craftsman house used to house the offices of the Santa Monica Conservancy. It is named in honor of Barbra Streisand's production company.

Winding Way

Pacific Coast Highway

SOUTH PARADISE COVE

PARADISE COVE AND ENVIRONS IN 2004. Paradise Cove was the home of director Blake Edwards and his wife Julie Andrews for many years. His spoof of the self-absorbed film community, *B.S.*, was filmed in his home and starred Andrews, William Holden, Robert Preston, Shelly Winters and Larry Hagman. Eschewing the traditional premiere venues, Edwards chose to premiere the movie at the modest Malibu Theater. As guests crossed the street to have dinner at La Scala, they were greeted by a very big black bull. The Edwards/Andrews property was later sold to Dodi Al-Fayed who died in the same crash that killed Diana, Princess of Wales.

Sycamore Park Tennis Courts

Pacific Coast Highway

Malibu Cove Colony

Latigo Point

MALIBU COVE COLONY AND LATIGO POINT

9

"Yes California, this is a Day of Days!

It is truly Italian—

a-dolce-far-niente-al-fresco-siesta day.

One ought not to speak English today."

—FREDERICK HASTINGS RINDGE

BIG DUME commands spectacular views of the coast and mountains. Along the wave-washed coast, where the crannies in the cliffs meet the shore, the thunder of the boisterous surf echoes on the mountainsides.

Point Dume, a barren, windswept promontory that rests on sandstone cliffs, has captured imaginations since its discovery by European explorers in 1793. British Captain George Vancouver was sent by the King of England to chart the Indian and Spanish villages along the California coast, and during the course of his exploratory voyage, he met Father Francisco Dumetz at Mission San Buenaventura. Together, they sailed down the coast and finally arrived at the spectacular point—latitude 33°/59.76, longitude 118°/48.26—on November 24, 1793. Vancouver named the point "Dumetz," for his traveling companion, and today it is called Point Dume.

Rumors of smuggling around the Point and its nestled beach coves have abounded since Spanish rule. According to records, Tiburcio Tapia, the prosperous merchant son of Bartolomé, allowed imported goods for his store to arrive at his family's private port of entry in Malibu, a practice prohibited by customs agents. (Smuggling became a common practice in these early days. Even Mathew Keller "imported goods" at his own landing place near today's pier, which became known as Keller's Shelter). Later, Frederick Rindge, who called the Point "Duma," wrote of detectives coming to the Malibu rancho to spy on opium dealers and smugglers of Chinese laborers. In fact, laborers were hidden in the caves at Semler Ranch. Still later, during the Prohibition years,

LITTLE DUME
"The atmosphere is so heavily charged with ozone as to make it a valuable tonic and strength builder."
—Frederick Hastings Rindge

bootleggers and rum-runners came ashore and hid their cargo in those same caves.

During World War II, Point Dume became a desirable armory primarily because of its views of the coast. The few barracks residents on the point added to the convoys to Point Mugu, and because of the Army personnel and the expectation, particularly after Pearl Harbor, that the war might spread to American soil, blackouts were strictly enforced on the coast. Even a lighted cigarette was a cause for concern.

After the war, the Point was flattened, subdivided into acre-sized lots by Marblehead Land Company, and sold with beach rights. To beautify the area, the National Park Service gave away trees for use as windbreaks, and the families who settled the Point built ranch houses, rode horses and used the beaches for fishing, diving and surfing. Pirates' Cove, a cozily recessed beach below the cliffs, became an attraction in the 1970s as a nude beach.

From the Point, the marvelous vista can include gray whales and their babies traveling north through Malibu on their long journey from Mexico to Alaska. And, of course, in the spring Malibu yellow abounds— fields of yellow coastal daisies mix with California poppies whose petals are a joyous yellow as wildflowers bloom all over the cliffs. Point Dume is California Historical Landmark No. 965.

AN ARTISTIC RETREAT. Artist, painter and sculptor Chuck Arnoldi and his wife, novelist Katie Arnoldi, live with their family on the cliffs, where they enjoy the Malibu lifestyle all year round—swimming, scuba diving, surfing, and dirt biking.

POINT DUME CLUB is owned by the Adamson family and is three hundred residents strong. The Point Dume Club and Paradise Cove, gated mobile-home parks complete with clubhouse, pool, spa and tennis court, are unlike most mobile-home parks. They are styled as Craftsman cottages, villas, and Hawaiian country homes with amenities such as hardwood floors, skylights, raised roofs, granite countertops and wrapped decks.

113

Grey Fox

LITTLE DUME

Westward
Beach

Cliffside Drive

Walking Trails

Vista
Point

Stairway to Beach —

Big Dume

POINT DUME HEADLANDS

Fernhill Drive

Bison Court

Grey Fox

Cliffside Drive

POINT DUME

10

"*Oh, the happy vaqueros!*

Who would be a banker,

when *he could ride the smiling hills*

and hide himself and his horse

in the tall mustard!"

—Frederick Hastings Rindge

THE REMUDA was a community equestrian event held
in the civic center for a few years in the 1940s.
Often a Malibu Colony resident celebrity, such as
June Lockhart or Warner Baxter, would lead the parade.

Traveling by horseback has a long tradition
among those who have lived in Malibu.
In 1776, Juan Bautista de Anza rode the coast
of California in his explorations, and later May
Rindge, with her *vaqueros* and guards, rode the

Malibu rancho. The 1940s saw the Gymkanna Ring,
where rodeos and 4-H events were held in
the civic center. In 1953, Percy Meek of the Mesa
Ranch founded Trancas Ropers and Riders.
The group's original riding ring was on the Pacific

MALIBU COWGIRL. At the age of twelve, Millie Meek Decker, along with her sister, rode a steer into the ring as the opening act on the rodeo circuit. Her father would ride to the rescue of the two girls, delighting the crowds. Since then, she has ridden in and won many trophies for her performances in horseshows, parades and fairs. Presently, she is writing her memoirs as a Malibu resident since 1925, and still lives up on Decker Road, named for her husband Jimmy's family. The Decker family pioneered ranching northwest of Malibu rancho in 1886, and because of them, there is a road down the canyon to the beach.

Coast Highway at Trancas. Its monthly shows, trail rides and square dances were all highly anticipated events. The Malibu Equestrian Center is now home to Trancas Ropers and Riders, and horses and riders still explore the trails which run throughout the hills and canyons. Eventually, of course, old horse trails of Rindge family days gave way to automobile roads, but the tradition of horseback riding is still part of the Malibu way of life.

RIDE TO THE HOUNDS IN MALIBU. Merz was a master horseman and led numbers of happy equestrians on trail rides through the canyons and along the beaches. He also organized fox hunts, riding to the hounds along Winding Way and through Escondido Canyon.

EGON MERZ is a legendary name in the equestrian circles of Malibu. In the summer of 1932, the Olympic Equestrian Games were held at the Riviera Polo Club, also known as Will Rogers State Park. The Riviera Riding Club was created on this site after the Games, and Egon Merz, a champion jumper, trained there and introduced dressage. Among his students were Claudette Colbert, Paulette Goddard, Jeanette MacDonald, Ray Milland, Mary Pickford, and Ronald Reagan. After picnicking on Escondido Beach in 1941, Merz bought property there and built his beloved Rancho Sea Air, where he moved his horses on the hill above the beach.

NATIONAL VELVET. Under Egon Merz's tutelage at his Malibu ranch, Elizabeth Taylor and her horse The Pie perfected her riding for her role in National Velvet (1944).

ESCONDIDO FALLS is the grand finale after a peaceful trail ride through Escondido Canyon. The serene grotto—on the private property of the heirs to the Dudley Murphy estate—is at its best after a rain.

To drive into the woodlands of Escondido Canyon, at whose head we come face to face with a great precipice of rock over which fall the Escondido Cataract. Escondido means "hidden," and this beautiful gem is indeed hidden away. Without a guide, you could never find it. On the face of the precipice, two white sulfur springs exude their waters, coloring the rock, while all about the pool are masses of Maidenhair fern, growing even up the sides of the cliff. A Sycamore tree bends over as in benediction. We leave this fernside, silent, until by mutual impulse we begin singing "Hiding in Thee."
—Frederick Hastings Rindge

11

"There is much virtue in beach sand.

It has excellent **strength-giving power**

for the weak."

—FREDERICK HASTINGS RINDGE

CALIFORNIA LIFEGUARDS from twenty-two agencies compete at Zuma Beach.

This lovely Zumaland lies close beside the sea. 'Tis the fairest valley of all those that grace these wonderlands. High mesas rise on either side guarding this nature's shrine. Great mountain crags form its background, while around the vale groves of branching sycamores, like sentinels . . . stand. Who but God could have wrought its beauteous site and curving hills? Fair Zumaland!

—FREDERICK HASTINGS RINDGE

THE SANDS OF ZUMA

Zuma comes from the Chumash word meaning "abundance," and indeed the long stretches of white sand and the steep hills behind it suggest nothing less than richness and fecundity.

In Zuma Canyon, along Bonsall Road, the site of Zuma Camp lay alongside the Rindges' Malibu rancho barns and corrals. Named for Howard Bonsall of Marblehead Land Company, the road leads to an equestrian and agricultural paradise. The tropical canyon also has a drive named for Louis Busch, who sold the canyon real estate.

Below the west-facing cliffs of the Point is beautiful and clean Westward Beach, which curves a mile northward to meet the white sands of Zuma. Where Zuma Creek meets the sea, there was once a marshland that housed a bird-hunting club. Guests of the club found a rich game area for duck, quail and pheasant.

THE WORLD OF ZUMA ORCHIDS. Only in Malibu' are the bank and post office filled with baskets of beautiful orchids. All because of world-renowned orchid grower Amado Vazquez, a master of hybridization. His career began in Malibu in 1950 when he worked with the orchids of MGM producer Arthur Freed, and decades later, he partnered with Dr. James McPherson to form Zuma Canyon Orchids. The Malibu fire of 1978 destroyed Zuma Canyon Orchids, but Vazquez prevailed. Left with just a handful of plants, he purchased the McPherson partnership share and rebuilt the business. Inside the greenhouses of Zuma Canyon Orchids, each blossom, every miraculous color is a tribute to Amado Vazquez.

When Los Angeles County acquired Zuma Beach after the Marblehead Land Company defaulted on taxes in 1941, officials razed homes that had been built on the beach and built a parking lot bordering the mile-and-a-half-long beach.

Malibu surfer Lance Carson recalls the beaches in Malibu: "Zuma was such a clean beach. The sands at Malibu, Zuma and Topanga were so white, clean and pure when I was growing up. At low tide, when the sand was slick after the water dried on it, I was able to take my bare feet and curl up my toes and skip the balls of my feet along the sand—and it would squeak. I mean, literally, squeak! When I would get out of the water, I would dive into the hot sand to dry off."

BROAD BEACH ROAD AT TRANCAS. This photo shows the old dirt road that Los Angeles County completed in 1921 and in the distance, Point Dume, before it was flattened.

COAST HIGHWAY AT TRANCAS. The new paved highway was a stone's throw from the houses on Zuma Beach before those homes were razed by the county in 1945 to make way for a parking lot.

MALIBU TRADING POST at Trancas was a destination for homesteaders from the north. There they would stock up on supplies. In 1921 a headline in the *Los Angeles Times* declared "Gold Discovered in Malibu" and the rush was on. Up Trancas Canyon, on the Kincaid Ranch, a gold mine was in operation to mine "flower gold." Inherent difficulties of mining in this canyon forced the mine out of business. Until the 1940s, the public phone at the Malibu Trading Post was the last phone to the north in Malibu. To call out, homesteaders had to dial only four digits. By the late 1960s, lower Trancas Canyon was developed as a residential tract, now called Malibu West.

THE LIGHTHOUSE AND BOATHOUSE were symbols of Hollywood in Malibu. Silent-film actress Pauline Frederick's lighthouse and her neighbor's houseboat were memorable sights on Trancas Beach in the 1930s. Pauline's best-known movie was *Madame X* (1920).

TRANCAS INN IN THE 1970s was a hangout for
The Band, Bob Dylan, The Eagles and Fleetwood Mac
when they were not on tour. Pictured here are bassist
Rick Danko and drummer Levon Helm of The Band.
They leased a ranch in Malibu and outfitted it with
a recording studio they called Shangri-La.

MALIBU PARK—FROM BEAN FIELDS TO GEHRY. The Marblehead Land Company leased the sloping hills of Malibu rancho in the 1930s and 1940s for dry farming—crops that could grow without irrigation, such as alfalfa, wheat, peas and lima beans. Tomato fields once covered the land on which Malibu High School stands. A far cry from the lima bean fields of the 1940s, artist Ron Davis's studio–residence reflects the sun in a metallic, trapezoidal architectural statement designed by architect Frank Gehry.

BROAD BEACH. North of Trancas is Broad Beach, a wide, sandy dune that curves out to Victoria Point. As sands do, there has been a southward movement at Broad Beach, and together with teardowns and rebuilds, the beach has been transformed from its earlier days.

VICTORIA POINT, at the end of Broad Beach, showcases a home, designed by famed Los Angeles modernist John Lautner. The Point was originally called Lachusa Point and was purchased by Paulette Goddard. She sold the property to Sidney Franklin, who renamed it Victoria Point in honor of his daughter.

EL MATADOR is the most famous of a cluster of three
beaches maintained by California State Parks—
El Matador, La Piedra and El Pescador—
along the picturesque Encinal Bluffs.

THE POTRERO AT CHARMLEE. The Spanish called this large, flat, mountain meadow *potrero*, and today the views of the Channel Islands from Charmlee Wilderness Park are breathtaking. Originally homesteaded by Marion Decker in 1885, Encinal Canyon was dynamited by Decker to create a wagon trail down to the beach. More than a half-century later, in the 1950s, after the land had passed through several hands, the Schwartzes named the meadow Charmlee (after their two first names, Charmian and Leon) and built a house, complete with swimming pool, on the property. In 1962, after a fire destroyed their home, the Schwartzes donated the land to the county for a park. The county bought additional acreage from Jud Roberts, who had owned an adjacent parcel since 1948. In 1999, the entire area was named Charmlee Wilderness Park and has been run by the City of Malibu Department of Parks and Recreation. Volunteer docents provide a full schedule of educational nature programs at Charmlee.

Juan Cabrillo Middle School

Malibu High School

Zuma Beach

ZUMA BEACH AND MALIBU PARK

Pacific Coast Highway

Broad Beach Road

Broad Beach

Encinal Canyon Road

Pacific Coast Highway

ENCINAL BLUFFS

12

*"On we rode, through picturesque cañons, **under the oaks,** until we emerged on fair Soston's peak.*

BONEY RIDGE. Created by an ancient lava flow, Boney Ridge at the north end of the Santa Monica Mountains has an almost magical quality. In the 1940s, shepherds and their herds populated the hillsides of Boney Ridge. As Frederick Hastings Rindge says, "It was in one of these cañons that we found the Grotto Beautiful, where the stalactites hang down in picturesque beauty. The lime formations make an arch above your head, while through the opening you look out upon the blue sky and green foliage of a Sycamore. In July the whole roof of the grotto is ablaze with a mass of bright yellow flowers. The water trickles down through the limestone, and in the hottest of days, coolness can be found. It is a steep descent to the grotto, but the sight is one of great variety and beauty."

From this summit are matchless marine and mountain views. We said there was **nothing human about that vista; it was divine.”**

—Frederick Hastings Rindge

HUNTERS IN NICHOLAS CANYON
are photographed with dogs.
Photo was taken in the 1940s.
Note the mountain lion.

Between Encinal Road and Decker Canyon is
Lachusa Canyon, named for a relative by marriage
of Don Bartolomé Tapia who was known as
"*La Chusa*." Water ran in the stream near their adobe year
round, and La Chusa grew vegetables and practiced tribal
medicine. The Tapia rancho became a favorite spot for
travelers as well as a hideaway for friends, primarily because
of the hospitality, but equally importantly, because one
could use the rancho as a lookout to see far down the
coast and determine if posses approached.

José Bartolomé Tapia hired Indians from the nearby Chumash village of Lisiqshi—now Leo Carrillo
Beach—to help tend his large herd of cattle and his vineyard.

Lisiqshi was the last occupied Chumash village,
abandoned around 1830, along the Santa Monica Bay.
Archeologists have dated significant artifacts from the site
as far back as seven thousand years.

Lisiqshi was later named Sequit or Seco, and the
canyon inland was called "Arroyo Sequit." Sequit Point
housed *vaqueros*, who worked the north end of Malibu
rancho, in a house and barn. In 1862, the Homestead Act

NICHOLAS FLAT in the upper Arroyo Sequit was the site of Mesa Ranch, owned by attorney Stewart Salisbury, left, and housing large herds of horses and cattle. Percy Meeks, founder of Trancas Ropers and Riders, was Salisbury's ranch foreman and lived on the property, where he raised and trained hunting dogs until 1971.

allowed homesteaders to lay claim to land no larger than one hundred sixty acres, pay a filing fee, improve the land and live on it for five years in order to be eligible to apply for a deed. Once the act was finalized in 1880, an influx of homesteaders converged on the Santa Monica Mountains. The National Park Service estimated that nearly sixteen hundred squatters and homesteaders tried to settle in the area, but only eight hundred succeeded. In upper Arroyo Sequit, westside settlers Harris and Guthrie built a wagon trail in 1884 to the beach trail at Malibu rancho and drove

a wagon through the ranch to Santa Monica.

To the north in 1886, Marion Decker and William Drake carved a private road down to the beach from Encinal Canyon. Nicholas Canyon's Nicholson Ranch was popular with hunters who camped in Sequit Canyon, and Frederick Rindge allowed the hunters to pass through his property, even giving them a key to the gate. Later, May Rindge's legal battle with the County of Los Angeles to keep her property private hinged on the easement established by her husband as a favor to the hunters.

THE MESA RANCH OR NICHOLAS FLAT is now part of the California State Parks system and adjoins Leo Carrillo parkland. At Nicholas Flat, the sounds of migrating birds and frogs echo in the peaceful pond setting. In the spring, the meadows turn a lush green sparked with masses of vivid wildflowers, and the pond blooms with water lilies. On the hill, mountain laurel, wild lilac and blue ceanothus cover the landscape, making the hiking trails around the ranch particularly breathtaking. The rock formations at the end of the pond offer spectacular ocean views. A hiking trail leads down to Leo Carrillo Beach.

THE POND AT MESA
RANCH is a natural spring
enlarged in 1954 to
provide a watering hole
for livestock. Surrounded
by boulders and lichen-
covered oak trees, the
pond falls off dramatically
to a steep canyon.

SEQUIT BEACH, or Secos Beach as it was known in the 1930s, is now called Leo Carrillo Beach. A Coast Guard Station was located here during the war years. The coast highway was paved in 1929, so travelers could venture to this distant beach for an outing, and not long afterward, moviemakers found it a perfect location for their films.

LEO CARRILLO. In 1952, the state purchased fifteen hundred acres of Arroyo Sequit beach from Waite Phillips, a Los Angeles businessman. During that time, Leo Carrillo, actor, equestrian and vaudeville entertainer, served on the state's Parks and Recreation Commission as a promoter of state parks. His great-grandfather had been provisional governor of California in 1837. In 1959, Will Rogers, Jr., who was also a commissioner, led a move to rename Sequit Beach "Leo Carrillo State Beach." Carrillo starred in the television series *Cisco Kid,* filmed over the hill at Paramount Ranch, from 1950 to1956, and later wrote a book entitled *The California I Love,* which featured a chapter on *La Chusa.* In his will, Carrillo left an endowment dedicated to the development and maintenance of Leo Carrillo State Park.

MALIBU ARCHITECT ED NILES designs residences which bring
the outdoors in. His own glass house nestles on the slope overlooking Leo Carrillo Beach very near where the last twig huts
of the Chumash tribe of Santa Monica Bay were situated.
Nearby, Nicholas Canyon drops to the Pacific Coast Highway.

WHEN ONSHORE WINDS BLOW, Leo Carrillo Beach is a favorite location for windsurfers with their colorful sails. Invented by local surfers Hoyle Schweitzer and Jim Drake in the 1960s, windsurfing caught on in the 1980s when a maneuverable short board was designed for windsailing, or windsurfing. Surfers refer to favorite surf spots in this area: "Secos," "County Line," "Zeros" and "Staircase."

Arroyo Sequit

SORTILEGIUM! ENCHANTMENT! Tony Duquette, an internationally acclaimed artist and interior designer as well as designer of stage sets and jewelry, built a retreat—which he called *Sortilegium!*—on fifty-five acres overlooking Boney Ridge. He built twenty-one structures on the property and gave them all names. His eclectic whimsical style and use of collectibles created a land of enchantment. Although all of the structures were destroyed in the fire of 1993, these photos document Duquette's masterpiece. At left is "Bosphorous," a domed structure with Boney Ridge as a backdrop. In the foreground is the giant twenty-eight-foot angel sculpture Duquette created as a tribute to the Los Angeles bicentennial.

THE GARDEN PAVILION AND PAGODA designed by Duquette reflect his cinematic style. At left, the pavilion is made from Navy surplus metal frames and the antlers were imported from the Hearst Ranch. The Tea House pagoda, above, is furnished in antique Chinese palace rugs, porcelains and Southeast Asian carvings. Duquette designed the chandelier.

SANDSTONE PEAK is the highest point in the Santa Monica Mountains at 3111 feet. At its base is Circle X Ranch which is located at the top of Yerba Buena Canyon. Here, the Backbone Trail leads to Sandstone Peak. Glorious 360-degree views at the top include the Channel Islands, Santa Monica Bay, the Conejo Valley and the San Fernando Valley. Frederick Rindge writes of hunting in Yerba Buena Canyon: "The Padres of San Gabriel used to send their Indians to the Malibu Ranch to fish and hunt, drying the fish and venison for a winter's supply. There, deer were very numerous; even in my time (1898), an old hunter related how, in Yerba Buena Cañon, he had killed forty-five deer."

"The golden glimmer of the Sunrise Sea

is of great beauty,

while the *sunsets supply*
    a public picture gallery
    at the close of countless days

        in the year."

—FREDERICK HASTINGS RINDGE

ACKNOWLEDGMENTS

While researching *Malibu* and finding some of the photos, both old and new, I have met and talked to some of the truly nicest and brightest people one ever hopes to know. Some have become friends and all have contributed in different ways to make this possible. To all, my love and thanks.

Many of the beautiful photographs is this book are the result of the magnificent eye of Nick Rodionoff. I extend my thanks to him for his glorious work.

I am very grateful to the gentle man, Ernest Marquez, for his marvelous old Malibu photos. Toni and Tom Doyle and Ron Rindge have been the historians who helped me make certain the facts are correct. My thanks go also to Deborah Miller, archivist of Malibu Lagoon Museum; film historian Dan Price; the sweet ladies Millie Meek Decker and her friend Helen Wilcox, who have many fond memories; Erin Murphy; the realty historians Louis Busch and Ann Rudy; the helpful bunch at the National Park Service—Phil Bedel, Patty Coleman and Phil Holmes; John Marin, Louis McCloud, Oralee and Ed Kewits and Bill Littlejohn for memories of The Colony; antique collector Doug Himmelfarb—thanks for the postcard. I am also grateful to my helpful dear friend, Sylvia Sheppard, for her expertise. A special thanks to all my family for their support. I am grateful to Paddy Calistro and Scott McAuley of Angel City Press for putting up with me and to the talented designer, Amy Inouye.

My special thanks, also to the following special people: Lauren and Jenny Aspell, Chuck and Katie Arnoldi, Barry Balin, Jennifer Bartle, Bill Beebe, Grant Brittian, Janice Burns, Capitol Records, Jon Christensen, Carolyn Conrad, Jean Crawford, Quant Carter, "just" Claire, Chris Cortezza, Tim Dion, Sally Evans, Johnny Fain, Marsha Feldman, Shirlee Fonda, Mary Gonzales, Susan Green, Paul Grisant, Ben Hall, Brendan Hearne, Glen Howell, Blake Jones, Jan Kachmer, Kathy Kohner, Frank Lamonea, Patty Lapinski, Peggy Lawyer, Michael and Kim McCarty, Kathy McGuire, Judy McKee, Judge John Merrick, Martha Nielsen, Joe Nonne, Jamie Padgett, Mary Ann Rea, Jud Roberts, Lisa Roberts, Molly Rubick, Steve Steere, Anneleis Steelenburg, Bob Stroms, Amado Vazquez, Rick Wallace, Jefferson Wagner, Hutton Wilkenson, Tricia Wilcox, Jane Wormhoudt, Arnold York and the Zuma Beach lifeguards.

COLONY TENNIS TOURNAMENT. Colony resident, animation artist and tennis player Bill Littlejohn's sign announced the Colony Tennis Tournament. He and Bob McCloud kept the ball in play for the Colony tennis players for four decades.

PHOTO CREDITS

Images in *Malibu* are the work of photographer Nick Rodionoff, unless credited below. The author and publisher gratefully acknowledge the following photographers, archives and individuals:

BIBLIOGRAPHY

Automobile Club of Southern California Archives. "The Malibu Run." *Touring Topics,* April 1910.

Beebe, Bill. "The Gentleman." *Santa Monica Outlook,* September 20, 1980.

Betsky, Aaron and Richard Barnes. *Three California Houses: The Homes of Max Palevsky.* New York: Rizzoli, 2003.

Beyette, Beverly. "Riding That Wave Again." *Los Angeles Times,* October 14, 2001.

California State Department of Parks and Recreation Southern Service Center. *Resource Element and General Plan, Leo Carrillo State Park.* San Diego: California State Department of Parks and Recreation, 1996.

Clary, William W. *History of the Law Firm of O'Melveny & Myers.* Los Angeles: O'Melveny & Myers, 1966.

Costin, Glynis. "The Other Malibu." *Women's Wear Daily,* August 7, 1989.

Darrach, Mike. "Malibu." *People,* August 1, 1983.

de Turenne, Veronique. "Upwardly Mobile Homes." *Los Angeles Times,* July 24, 2003.

Doyle, Thomas W. *The Malibu Story,* Malibu: Malibu Lagoon Museum, 1985.

Fischer, Carla. "By the Sea, by the Sea, by the Beautiful Sea." *Malibu Monthly Magazine,* December 2003.

Fox, Patti. "Malibu Resident Upholds Western Traditions." *Malibu Surfside News,* January 2004.

Ghini, John. "Villa Leon." *Malibu Lagoon Newsletter,* 1999.

Giovanni, Joseph. "On Light and Lines." *Architectural Digest,* December 2002.

Grant, Campbell. *The Rock Paintings of the Chumash.* Berkeley and Los Angeles: University of California Press, California, 1965.

Groves, Martha. "Old Malibu Pier Catches a Wave." *Los Angeles Times,* March 7, 2003.

Hamilton, Sara. "Mad, Merry, Malibu." *Photoplay,* September 1932.

Howell, Glen. "May Knight Rindge." *Malibu Lagoon Newsletter,* 2005.

Huntington Library Archives. Matthew Keller Papers. San Marino, California: The Huntington Library, Art Collections, and Botanical Gardens, 2003.

Jaffe, Matthew. "Big Changes in the Santa Monica Mountains." *Sunset,* February, 1994.

Kampion, Bruce. *Stoked! A History of Surf Culture.* Santa Monica: General Publishing, 1997.

Lightwood, Carol. *Malibu.* Malibu: Malibu Books, 1984.

Littlejohn, Bill. "Colony Directors Indicted." *Malibu Colony Variety,* September 1974.

Lynch, Gary and Malcolm Gault-Williams. *Tom Blake: the Uncommon Journey of a Pioneer Waterman.* Corona del Mar, California: Croul Family Foundation, 2001.

Malibu Chamber of Commerce. "Paradise Cove." Malibu: Malibu Chamber of Commerce, 1952.

Malibu High School Honors Class. *An Oral History of The Malibu.* Malibu: Malibu High School, 1997.

Marcus, Ben. "In Jay's Hands." *Malibu Monthly Magazine,* October 2003.

McAuley, Milt. *Hiking Trails of the Santa Monica Mountains.* Canoga Park, California: Canyon Publishing, 1980.

Merrick, John. "Maritime Stories of Point Dume and Malibu." *Malibu Times,* January 2001.

— *History of Malibu.* Malibu: Malibu Books, 1984.

Miller, Bruce W. *Chumash, A Picture of Their World.* Los Osos, California: Sand Review Press, 1988.

National Park Service, Cultural Resource Staff. "Solstice Canyon: Keller House, Its True Origin." *National Park Service Cultural Resource Newsletter,* 2004.

O'Quinn, Ryan. "Debate Heats Up Over Steelhead, Rindge Dam." *Malibu Times,* July 2, 2003.

— "Shipwrecked Yacht 'Malibu' Gets $2.4 Million Overhaul." *Malibu Times,* September 9, 2003.

Rindge, Frederick H. *Happy Days In Southern California.* Los Angeles: Anderson, Richie and Simon, 1898.

Rindge, Ronald L. *World War II Homeland Defense: U.S. Coast Guard Beach Patrol in Malibu, 1942-1944.* Cayucos, California: Ron and Sue Rindge, 2003.

Robinson, Joe. "Pushing Sixty: the Miles Add Up for the Backbone Trail." *Los Angeles Times,* March 23, 2004.

Robinson, William Wilcox and Lawrence Clark Powell. *The Malibu, Southern California's Famous Rancho, Its Romantic History and Present Charm.* Los Angeles: Ward Ritchie Press, 1958.

Rouse, Reverend Warren J. *The Franciscans at Serra Retreat Since 1942.* Malibu: Serra Retreat, 2002.

Semler, Ronnie. *A Narrative of Saddlerock Ranch.* Malibu: Saddlerock Ranch, 2004.

Shaw, David. "The New Stars of Malibu: Winemakers." *Los Angeles Times,* July 16, 2003.

Soble, Anne. "Corral Canyon Trailhead Dedicated." *Malibu Surfside News,* August 2003.

Stingle, John. "Malibu Deal Marks Era in Coast Realty." *Los Angeles Examiner,* November 25, 1928.

Wallack, Ray. "King of the Thrill: Trapeze of the Seas." *Los Angeles Times,* December 16, 2003.

Weiss, Kenneth. "The Sand and the Fury in Malibu." *Los Angeles Times,* July 10, 2004.